What readers are saying about *A Lens On America*:

"A unique view, from a travel insider who understands the importance of the journey."

— *William Hamm,*
Prescription Management Industry Leader

"A captivating and entertaining journey across North America."

— *Kristin Arnold,*
Founder of the Extraordinary Team,
National Speaker, & Award Winning Author

"Personal insight, funny stories, and deep history brought to life in these wonderful tales from the road."

— *Phillip Speligene,*
Field Support Manager
Yamaha Motor Corporation. U.S.

"*A Lens On America* is a great blend of history, memorable sites and the people you meet along the way."

— *Donna Paulson,*
Tour Director

"Wonderfully informative and magnificently presented. The magnitude of information prepares the would be traveler, for the ultimate experience."

— *Tom & Nikki Sharp,*
Social Media Experts & Authors

"This book, *A Lens on America,* is an excellent utensil for planning your next adventure, combining interesting facts, photographs and precious memories. It's as though you are engaging in a conversation with an extremely knowledgeable and humorous tour guide. I thoroughly enjoyed this book!"
  —*Linzie McCullough, Histotechnologist*

"Isley's depiction of the geography of the United States and Americana from a personal perspective provides a unique insight that leaves the reader wanting to seek an adventure all their own."
  —*Travis White, Attorney*

2nd EDITION

A Closer Look at Key State Facts

&

What the Family Learned Along the Way

Arlie Isley
with *Kelly Isley*

A Lens On America
Arlie's Journey Across 50 States
A Closer Look At Key State Facts & What The Family Learned Along The Way

Copyright © 2016 by B&IB Publishers
Contact: Kellyisley.the.author@gmail.com
www.ALensOnAmerica.com

World rights reserved. No part of this publication may be reproduced, stored in a retrieval system or transmitted, in any form or by any means, electronic, mechanical, photocopying, recording or otherwise for public use, including Internet applications, without the prior permission of the author except by a reviewer who may quote brief passages in a review to be printed in a magazine, newspaper or on the Web.

Published by B&IB Publishers
Scottsdale, Arizona

Library of Congress Cataloging-in-Publication Data
Isley, Arlie with Isley, Kelly   A Lens On America   - Arlie's Journey Across 50 States

Hardcover: ISBN 978-0-9887518-7-3
Softcover: ISBN 978-0-9887518-8-0
eBook: ISBN 978-0-9887518-2-8

Book design by Kurt Wahlner
La Conchita, California; www.wahlner.com

Part of the Tree Neutral® program, which offsets the number of trees consumed in the production and printing of this book by taking proactive steps, such as planting trees in direct proportion to the number of trees used: www.treeneutral.com

Manufactured in the United States of America
Second Edition

DEDICATION

To my remarkable

growing family

★ ACKNOWLEDGEMENTS ★

While writing this book, my Dad and I agreed on two things: first that a book is a present you can open again and again, second that there are many acknowledgements due when a book represents several decades of travel, passion, and experience.

With that, we are sending special thanks to Norma Isley, Henry Benjes III, Kurt Wahlner, Kelly Youngblood, Kristin Arnold, Mary Ann Zimmerman, and many others who have made tremendous contributions to *A Lens On America*.

CONTENTS

Introduction / 9

Alabama / 13

Alaska / 19

Arizona / 28

Arkansas / 38

California / 43

Colorado / 48

Connecticut / 59

Delaware / 63

Florida / 68

Georgia / 75

Hawaii / 80

Idaho / 87

Illinois / 93

Indiana / 100

Iowa / 105

Kansas / 110

Kentucky / 115

Louisiana / 121

Maine / 129

Maryland / 137

Massachusetts / 143

Michigan / 149

Minnesota / 156

Mississippi / 162

Missouri / 169

Montana / 175

Nebraska / 183

Nevada / 189

New Hampshire / 194

New Jersey / 199

New Mexico / 205

New York / 212

North Carolina / 221

North Dakota / 227

Ohio / 232

Oklahoma / 240

Oregon / 250

Pennsylvania / 256

Rhode Island / 263

South Carolina / 272

South Dakota / 277

Tennessee / 283

Texas / 290

Utah / 296

Vermont / 304

Virginia / 310

Washington / 320

West Virginia / 328

Wisconsin / 333

Wyoming / 342

Washington, D.C. / 350

Appendix / 357

Bibliography / 359

About the Authors / 360

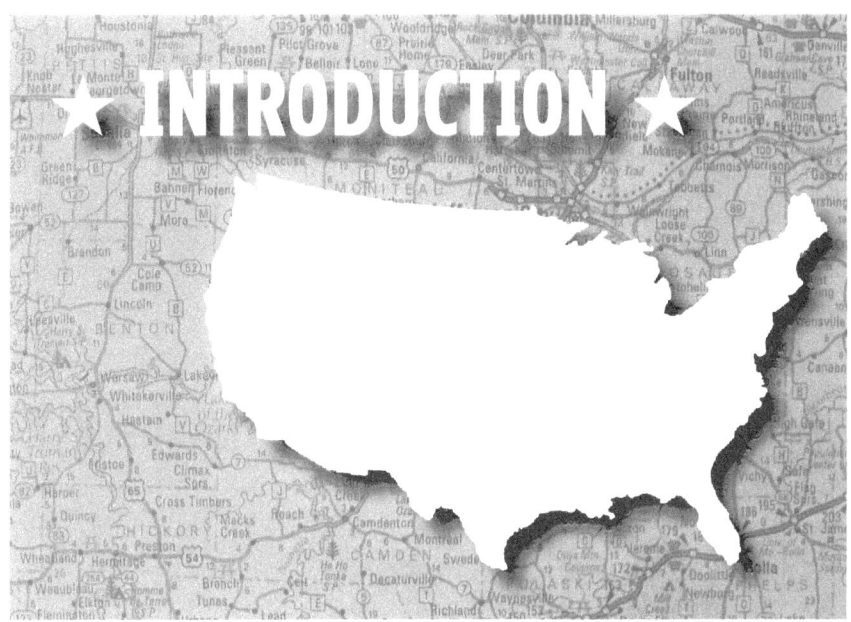

My desire to travel began at a very early age, when my dad took me on a trip to Colorado. I was only eight years old and I was hooked. After that first trip, when I was invited to go anywhere, I would go if my parents allowed me. On one occasion, a farmer neighbor who was hauling a load of castor beans to the nearest processing plant approximately 140 miles away asked if I wanted to ride along. I said yes. The old farm truck was slow and rough but I enjoyed the trip. I was willing to go on every trip to church camp or anywhere else, as long as it was an out of town adventure.

As I went through high school I began to think there must have been some gypsy blood in my ancestry. What could cure this restless nomadic nature? I didn't want to become a vagabond, a wanderer who drifts from place to place.

After high school, I was lucky enough to get a job with the U.S. Forest Service in Montana. This 2000 mile trip away from home helped satisfy my traveling desires for the time being. After the Forest Service job, I returned home and enlisted in the U.S. Army. This gave me the opportunity to travel to places such as Korea and Japan. After three years in the service, I started college and worked and received the G.I. Bill to support my college efforts.

By the time I graduated college, I was employed full time at a large corporation. I enjoyed college much more than my high school years. I thought that if I was to travel the way I wanted, I would need at least one degree in geography. I have always been curious to know what is over the next hill or around the next bend in the road. This degree in geography helped me understand much of the world we live in before I had the chance to experience it for myself.

While working at the corporation, I knew we would have to save financially and plan for an early retirement. We followed our plan and when the time was right, we retired very early. At the retirement party, one of the corporate directors asked me if I really wanted to do this and I answered with a definite "Yes!" He said, "Arlie, you are the only boy that ever retired from this corporation."

This early retirement allowed us precious time we needed to finish our traveling and exploring goals. Before retirement, we traveled as much as time would allow, but only four weeks of vacation each year is restrictive. For several years, we had condo time shares in different parts of the country and at the social parties the number one question was "what is your favorite state?" The answer was always the same: "we like them all!" Colorado is very different than Florida and Arizona is very different from New York. This infinite variety of culture, history, and climate makes life throughout these United States interesting and exciting.

Travel has fascinated people for centuries and now that we have the modern airplane, it is much easier and more convenient for people to be world travelers if they desire. We have been fortunate to have done it all. But our own wonderful country is the most fascinating for us. We have used motor homes, travel trailers, trains, automobiles, and commercial airlines to travel and explore the fifty states. It has all been a pleasure. I'm not much to give unsolicited advice, but don't miss those serendipitous side roads by flying too much. We have traveled several hundred thousand miles of road travel and have found many pleasant and unexpected surprises.

What I have learned through the "lens" of my own experience is that too many of my friends and acquaintances have waited too long to begin their travels. What I say to them, and others, is to not let life be just a destination; let it be a journey.

The German playwright, Goethe, said it best: "Whatever you can do or dream you can do, begin it. Boldness has genius, power, and magic in it. Begin it now."

Enjoy the journey,

Arlie

Arlie E. Isley, Author
A Lens On America

State Capital: Montgomery

State Flower: Camellia

Population: 4,779,736 (Ranks 23rd, as of 2010 Census)

Land Area: 50,645.3 square miles (Ranks 28th)

Population Density: 94.4 persons per square mile (Ranks 27th)

Arlie's Insight & Highlights

Alabama is also known as the "Heart of Dixie" and sometimes known as the Yellowhammer State. This is a nickname that originated during the Civil War, when some Alabama troops marched in uniforms trimmed in bright yellow cloth. The soldiers reminded the citizens of the Yellowhammer bird.

Alabama has a variety of geographic features, from Gulf Coastal Plains to the Appalachian Mountains. In the Appalachian Ridge area minerals such as coal, iron ore, and limestone are found. This mixture of minerals is used to make iron and steel. Birmingham is near the center of the geographic area and accounts for its great production of iron and steel industries. The other parts of the state are diversified in products. The Black Belt area is somewhat unique and was named for its black clay soils. In the 1860's farmers developed large plantations in this area but later it was infected by the boll weevils that forced the farmers to change to other crops and livestock. However, Alabama is still a leading cotton producing state, along with other crops of corn, peanuts and soy beans.

Some of Alabama's early history was a series of turbulent events. The first permanent settlement in the state was Fort Louis, on the Mobile River in 1702, by the French-Canadians. The settlement later moved south to the Mobile area. In 1814, General Jackson fought with the Creek Indians and defeated them in the Battle at Horseshoe Bend. Later the Creeks ceded about half of present-day Alabama to the United States.

In 1819, Alabama became the 22nd state in the union. Alabama seceded from the union on January 11, 1861 and became "The Republic of Alabama" until February 8, 1861, when it joined the Confederacy. The first capital of the Confederacy States was at Montgomery in 1861 and Jefferson Davis was inaugurated as the Confederate President there. One famous battle of the Civil War was the Battle of Mobile Bay on August 5, 1864, when one of the last ports of the confederacy was closed to shipping and trade. This was known as one of the "Red Letter" days of the conflict between the states. One other piece of history, important to African Americans was the founding of the Tuskegee Institute by the state in 1881 and was directed, until 1915, by Booker T. Washington, a former slave. Alabama was readmitted to the Union on June 25, 1868.

There are many places to visit and things to do in the state of Alabama. We enjoyed the *U.S.S. Alabama* (battleship *Alabama*) in Mobile Bay, which was presented to the state by the U.S. Government in 1964. It was one of many battleships that served in World War II. Other places of great interest are: the Space and Rocket center in Huntsville, where a large collection of missiles and space equipment are located, the first Capital of the Confederacy, in Montgomery and the first "White House" of the Confederacy, also in Montgomery, which was the home of President and Mrs. Jefferson Davis in the first months of the confederacy.

Alabama has some special events that stand out over all others, one of which is the Mardi Gras celebration in Mobile. Full of color and energy, this event generally occurs in February, and is followed by the beautiful blossoms which come along in late March or early April. This is a great time to visit our favorite spot just outside Mobile: the Bellingrath Gardens. We marveled at the fact that this 65 acre Garden Estate is in full bloom with camellias in the winter, azaleas in the spring, roses in the summer, chrysanthemums in autumn, and stunning Christmas lights during the holiday season. Next, in northwest Alabama is the Natchez Trace Parkway. It runs between Natchez, Mississippi and Nashville, Tennessee. This parkway is a historic route used by boatmen to go north after floating down the Mississippi River.

Other areas of interest and of historical value are located just south of the Bellingrath Home & Gardens. One can find Ft. Gains and Ft. Morgan National Historic Landmark, all in the general area of Dauphin Island and Mobile Bay. This waterway is found along the U.S. Gulf Coast and on the Atlantic Coast as well. It provides a navigable route along its length without the general hazards of travel on the open seaways.

★ Kelly's Perspective & Lessons Learned ★

Based on career experience, aerospace and aviation are the first two things that come to mind when I think of my visits to Alabama. Good examples of past destinations and how the state has supported these industries include: NASA's Marshall Space Flight Center, Huntsville's designation as the rocket capital of the world, and milestones involving Alabama workers who built the first rocket to put humans on the moon.

Continuing with tradition, in July 2014, Auburn University announced it will be elevating its aviation program by establishing a center to serve as a focal point for instruction and research, together with outreach, in support of the aviation and aerospace industries.

Famous People Born in Alabama

Henry Louis (Hank) Aaron the baseball player, born in Mobile in 1934.

Tallulah Brockman Bankhead the actress, born in Huntsville inn 1902.

Nat "King" Cole the entertainer, born in Montgomery in 1919.

Emmy Lou Harris the singer, born in Birmingham in 1947.

Kate Jackson the actress, born in Birmingham in 1948.

Percy Lavon Julian the inventor, born in Montgomery in 1899.

Helen Adams Keller the author, educator, born in Tuscumbia in 1880.

Joe Louis the boxer, born in Lafayette in 1914.

Willie Mays the baseball player, born in Westfield in 1931.

Jim Nabors the actor, born in Sylacauga in 1930.

Jesse Owens the athlete, born in Oakville in 1913.

Rosa Parks the civil rights activist, born in Tuskegee in 1913.

Heather Whitestone a previous Miss America, born in Dothan in 1973.

Hank Williams the recording artist, born in Mount Olive in 1923.

★ Where Will You Visit? ★

_____
_____
_____
_____

★ What Photos Will You Take? ★

_____
_____
_____
_____

State Capital: Juneau

State Flower: Forget-me-not

Population: 710,231 (Ranks 47th, as of 2010 Census)

Land Area: 570,641.0 square miles (Ranks 1st)

Population Density: 1.2 persons per square mile (Ranks 50th)

Arlie's Insight & Highlights

I feel sure that the Johnny Horton record, "North to Alaska" inspired many wondering travelers "to go in that direction."

We played that record many times before we took our first trip to the great state of Alaska.

On the first trip to this northern state, we flew to Anchorage, leased two motor homes (one for our journey and another for rancher friends) and stocked them with food before heading to Fairbanks. Between the friends, fishing, and the breathtaking setting, this turned out to be a joyful journey. Some of the first cities and towns we enjoyed on this northern route included Wasilla and Palmer. Sometime later, we camped at Montana Creek to fish for several types of salmon and trout.

We proceeded farther up the road to Willow and beyond, until we reached Denali National Park & Preserve, where we spent two days enjoying Mt. McKinley, the highest point in North

America at 20,320 feet, along with all of the wildlife in this scenic area. This National Park is one destination where one can experience the continent's highest peaks and extensive, unspoiled wilderness while viewing moose, caribou, Dall sheep, wolves, and grizzly bears in their natural habitat.

Going north to Denali Park, we came to the town of Nenana, where we stayed for a time to pan for gold and visit with the natives.

After arriving in Fairbanks, we spent considerable time exploring the city and taking in the sights which made it a great experience.

Our next stop took us southeast to North Pole, Alaska. This is the place where locals claim the mythical man in red, known as Santa Claus, is rumored to live and work with several helpers. We enjoyed this place of fantasy and it inspired us to shop for the holidays.

We continued south to Delta Junction, then on to Summit Lake and Paxson, stopping to fish and enjoy the mountain scenery. Heading on south we came to a small place known as Sourdough, Alaska. This was a great place to relax and fish for Grayling, which is a beautiful species of fish that appears to have wings. Before departing we took a number of photos and then headed south to Glennallen, Palmer and then into the Matanuska Valley which was bustling with activity.

While in Matanuska Valley, we learned it is Alaska's most productive farmland. Although the growing season is short, it is known for world-record sized cabbages, as well as other vegetables that are proudly displayed at the Alaska State Fair in Palmer. We departed this lush farmland to make our final trek to Anchorage. Upon arrival, we checked in the motor homes, shared the extra groceries with the men in the service department, and caught our flight home. Once we were settled on the plane, we knew that we had completed a memorable journey.

This journey was so thought-provoking that it would bring us back to Alaska several years later.

This time we decided to pull our travel trailer with a large Chevrolet Suburban. After mapping out our route, we decided to journey up the Alcan Highway, through Western Canada. The trip really began in Winnipeg, Manitoba, then the road took us west through Saskatchewan into Alberta, through northern British Columbia, into Yukon Territory and finally to the Alaskan Border.

Before leaving Yukon Territory, and the City of Whitehorse, Capital of Yukon, there is a trip to the Alaskan Pan Handle to Skagway, Alaska that is a memorable borough. The history of this area is nationally known. The White Pass out of Skagway was used by gold seekers heading up to the Klondike Region of the Yukon Territory in 1897-98 and later. The side trip turned out to be one of those true serendipitous side roads off the main path. To miss this side trip would have been a gross mistake. At the Klondike Gold Rush National Historical Park, we could see videos and photos of how excitement and adventure can turn into tragedy and sadness, where men and horses lost their lives, seeking the precious yellow metal.

As we proceeded up the Alcan Highway, we entered the main body of Alaska, near Tetlin Junction and Tok. Here at Tok, we attended and enjoyed a large salmon bake. After departing, we took the Tok cut-off, heading southwest to Glennallen, after resting here for a time, we continued toward Palmer, down the Matanuska Valley.

Our main goal for this visit was to explore and enjoy the southern part of Alaska and the Kenai Peninsula. After arriving in

Anchorage, we headed south to the Kenai Peninsula, to visit all the cities/towns of the area.

In Seward, Alaska we fished for King Salmon and other species that were available at that time of year.

From Seward, we went to Soldotna and Kenai, where we spent two weeks. During the first portion of our stay, I found myself fishing the Great Kenai River and also the Russian River on Father's Day. These were two rivers full of exciting spots for Sockeye fishing. The success we had in the Soldotna Area was fantastic for King Salmon fishing. We hired guides on the Kena River and headed down stream to College Hole. The large number of boats there might remind someone of the "Spanish Armada", which included 150 ships and at the time was the largest fleet ever seen in Europe.

As we approached the area, I noticed the boats were so close on College Hole that tensions were high and causing some fisherman to throw sinkers at each other's boats - due to the density. Additionally, a great deal of unsportsmanlike conduct was unfolding and included colorful exchanges. In spite of all of the excitement, I caught my largest King Salmon to date – which was a 53 pounder!

From this location, we moved down the peninsula, through a handful of scenic small towns: Kasilof, Clam Gulch, Ninilchik, and Anchor Point, continuing on down Sterling Highway, to Homer, Alaska. We camped at Homer for more than two weeks, which gave us a chance to go deep sea fishing for halibut in the Gulf of Alaska. My wife, Norma ended up catching the largest halibut and we both captured a few sea run Dolly Varden, which are highly sought after by anglers throughout Alaska. This was another reason it was a special time for both of us.

It was clear that our second visit to Alaska was a very productive fishing trip as well. Overall, we caught four of the five major species of Pacific Salmon. The one species we missed was the Silver (CoHo) Salmon, as they run late.

Other activities in Homer included special boat trips and tours. One trip was so surprising and memorable, I classified it as the serendipitous side trip of our second month out. This particular boat trip took us where no roads could go – into the charming waterfront community of Seldovia. Known as one of Alaska's best kept secrets, Seldovia's remote location makes it accessible only by boat or float plane. Intrigued by what would draw a person to this destination, we visited with many of the residents (255 total based on 2010 census) and learned that the population included artists, writers, and seclusion-seekers that wanted to live in peace and tranquility.

After returning to Homer, it was time to retrace our path back home. On the way, we returned to Wasilla and Palmer, before going back to Glennallen to take our last big side trip to the city of Valdez. The route south to Valdez, took us along the path of the great Trans-Alaska Pipeline. After our arrival, we had an exciting time exploring the area and fishing for Pink (Humpback) Salmon. We caught so many of these species we were tired each evening. Following the fishing we had one final

tour planned to the Valdez Oil Terminal, where the ships load oil to go down to the lower 48 states. We learned that the point of entry is at the local airport in a high security area. After going through a screening and security briefing we embarked on an interactive tour where we learned that an average of three to five oil tankers depart from the terminal each week. Since the pipeline began operating in 1977, more than 15,000 tankers full of oil have left the terminal.

One additional visit that will always remind me of Alaska includes our visit to Wasilla to see the history of the Iditarod. Known as the last great race on earth by many that attend and participate, the Iditarod's rich history is showcased at The World's Greatest Dog Sled Race headquarters in Wasilla.

After retracing our route down the Alcan Highway of the largest state in our union (e.g., more than twice the size of Texas), we arrived at our home in Oklahoma in late August. When we pulled in the driveway and checked our odometer showing 12,227 miles – it was clear that we had completed an amazing and unforgettable journey.

★ Kelly's Perspective & Lessons Learned ★

After reading this chapter, I am looking forward to heading north to Alaska!

★ Famous People Born in Alaska ★

Margaret Elizabeth Bell the author, born in Thorne Bay in 1898.

Benny Benson designed state flag at age 13, born in Chignik during 1913.

Chad Bentz the baseball pitcher, born in Seward in 1980.

Carlos Boozer NBA basketball player, born in Juneau in 1982.

Matt Carle Nation Hockey League player, born in Anchorage in 1984.

William A. Egan first state governor, born in Valdez in 1914.

Ray Mala the actor, born in Candle in 1906.

Curt Schilling the baseball pitcher, born in Anchorage in 1966.

Dave Williams the baseball pitcher, born in Anchorage in 1979.

Where Will You Visit?

What Photos Will You Take?

State Capital: Phoenix

State Flower: Saguaro blossom

Population: 6,392,017 (Ranks 16th, as of 2010 Census)

Land Area: 113,594.1 square miles (Ranks 6th)

Population Density: 56.3 persons per square mile (Ranks 33th)

★ Arlie's Insight & Highlights ★

When I think of Arizona, I remember the many visits I have had to this state. Before I recall the many journeys, it would be appropriate to review a short bit of history. In 1886, the Apache leader, Geronimo, surrendered to the U.S. Army and Arizona's Indians fighting had ended. Arizona, like many other territories, had long struggles before becoming part of the Union. However, in February of 1912, Arizona became the 48th state in the United States of America. This late arrival makes Arizona one of our newest states. As recently as 1948, the Arizona Indians received the right to vote. This was a milestone for these Native Americans, since Arizona has more Native Americans than any other state, except Oklahoma.

I feel privileged to have traveled from one corner of Arizona to the other, literally from Yuma in the southwest to the "Four Corners" in the northeast and from Douglas, in the southeast corner, to Boulder Dam in the northwest corner. As far as footprint, Arizona ranks 6th in size. The "Four Corners" area is where Arizona, Colorado, New Mexico, and Utah meet. This is the only place in the U.S. where a person can stand in four states at the same time.

Glen Canyon Dam, on the northern border and on the Colorado River, creates Lake Powell, and also turns the generators that create much needed hydroelectric power. On down the Colorado River is the Grand Canyon National Park that runs many miles., This river has created one of the seven natural wonders of the world. It is famous worldwide; on one of our trips there, we encountered people from several foreign countries who were awed by this spectacular sight. The Grand Canyon has easy access from Flagstaff or Williams, off I-40. The most fun was to stay at Williams, Arizona and catch a special train to the Grand Canyon. We got a real surprise on this trip. The train was "held up" by bandits and we were robbed, as if we were in the "Old West."

As we continue down the Colorado River, to Lake Mead and Boulder Dam, one can find many exciting sights at the Lake Mead Recreation Area.

If you travel on down this river, you will find the Davis Dam creates Lake Mohave. This is near the Bullhead City area. Across

from this city is Laughlin, Nevada, an oasis in the desert, which has lots of gaming. About 50 miles down the Colorado River, is another spot of beauty, Lake Havasu City, which is a unique place with the Old London Bridge, great shopping and sightseeing. On down the river, on the California border, is Yuma, Arizona. It has some nice camping areas along the river and the old Arizona Territorial Prison in located there.

If you travel across northern Arizona on I-40, there are several places of interest a short distance off the highway. First, from the east, is the Petrified Forest National Park and the Painted Desert on the north side of I-40, is a nice stop for families and grandchildren. Further west is the Meteor Crater, an interesting and mysterious sight. It is a large hole in the ground where a large object from space struck and went so deep the object has not been found. Continuing on to the west, is Flagstaff, Arizona, this place holds many interesting sights. One can see the Walnut Canyon National Monument, the Sunset Crater Volcano National Monument, the Oak Creek Canyon area and the Arizona Snow Bowl. A few miles south of Flagstaff is Sedona, a place well known by artists and writers, which is also a place of great natural beauty. Going south from Sedona, toward Phoenix, is the Montezuma Castle National Monument and 30 miles on down the road, is Agua Fria National Monument.

South of the Phoenix area is the location of Casa Grande Ruins National Park. As we travel on to the Tucson area, there are many great sites to visit.

Two major attractions are the Pima Air and Space Museum and Old Tucson Studios. For those interested in aircraft, this Pima Museum is the greatest that I have ever seen, in any of the 50 states. In Old Tucson, many films and parts of films have been shot. This visit will take one back to what the Old West was like. Other interesting places to see would include the Arizona-Sonora Desert Museum, west of Tucson and the Saguaro National Park. The Saguaro National Park extends east of Tucson. Southwest of Tucson is the San Xavier del Bac Mission. This is one of the best preserved of Arizona's early missions. It still has old painting and other displays. North of Tucson, is a strange structure, known as the biosphere, near Oracle. The biosphere is an outer-space dream, as this facility is completely self contained, providing food, water, and air to all inhabitants. Leaving visitors feeling it could be located anywhere in the cosmos.

In southeastern Arizona, between Benson and Bisbee, is the town of Tombstone. This is an old boom town where Wyatt Earp became famous as a gunfighter. When we stayed there, we met visitors from many places around the country. Don't miss the gunfight reenactments held there and be sure to see the cemetery.

Arizona has many Indian Reservations, some are well known and very large. Most that we have visited are in the northern and eastern parts of Arizona. The Navajo and Hopi are in the northeastern part, where one finds many other sites and landmarks. Monument Valley, Canyon de Chelly National Monument, Hubbell Trading Post National Historic Site and Navajo National Monument are all located in this general area. Farther south, the Zuni Indians have a smaller reservation. Two of the best known in eastern Arizona are Fort Apache Indian Reservation and the San Carlos Apache Indian Reservation. This area is much different than the arid northeastern corner of the state. If I had to choose a place to live, the latter two would be my first choice.

Most of my early experience in Arizona occurred in the Phoenix, Mesa, and Apache Junction area. This is where friends and relatives have lived for many years. My brother-in-law, Bob, had a magnificent obsession about finding gold in the Superstition

Mountains more specifically, the Lost Dutchman Mine. One of my first trips into Superstition Mountain's, was by horseback. We picked up two horses in Socorro, New Mexico and headed west, through Arizona, at night. All was going well, until we come into the Salt River Canyon area. We had a two horse trailer and the partition between the horses was not very high and one horse got a front foot across on the other side in the second horse's stall and could not get it back. It was a mad scramble for a while and the horses were mad! Finally, Bob helped the offending horse to get its leg back on the proper side. Thanks to Bob's strength and courage, we were on our way again.

My first trip into the mountains was eerie and full of suspense. Bob had been here several times before, so he knew where we could find water for the horses. Most of the year it's too hot

and dry for horses, but this trip was in early spring. I got my first introduction to an old mountain recluse, who had been in these mountains for more than twenty years. We had our own sleeping bags, but we would sleep near his camp. We knew there were rattlesnakes in the area, but we never encountered any of this dreaded species.

The first trip was a great adventure, but no gold was found. Bob worked at this project in his spare time through the years. Two years later, I accompanied Bob on a short trip into the Superstitions again, it was a hike-in trip, uneventful, and no gold found. In the mean time, Bob spent much time still searching for this Lost Dutchman Mine. Sometime during his searching, he found an interesting location where he spent time blasting and digging. He invited me to this location but said it was rugged and it had difficult access. I found out later what the word "rugged" meant. We went to the general area and began to climb. As we got near, we had to go along what was a long and narrow ridge. On previous visits, Bob had tied more than a 100 ft. of rope to hold on to, and we could look down either side several feet. After clearing this hurdle and going downhill for a while we approached the dig site. The dig site was a hole about 25 feet across and approximately 30-35 ft. deep. To go down the hole, we had to use a long rope. Bob went down first and I followed, but on my trip down, the rope twisted and I managed to tear a large piece of skin off my left hand. Bob had some band-aids so we patched me up a bit and we dug a while, ate lunch, dug some more, but no gold was found.

From this trip, we went home tired and hungry. I think in retrospect, this was my first inoculation for the Gold Fever.

The following year I was invited to go into the Superstitions' one more time. This time Bob had invited a mining engineer and an insurance executive, both from Colorado, and they both bought their wives along. All six of us went into the mountains, and stayed near the same camp as before. By this time there were many people coming in to stake claims and search for gold. Many carried guns and looked scary and unfriendly. We explored and searched on this trip, but did not go to Bob's dig site, it was too tough for some of the group's members. On the way out, one of the couples in front of Bob and me almost had a serious altercation. This trip was my final inoculation for the gold fever.

I miss seeing the Desert Flora in spring time; it has a special beauty in the blooming of the Palo Verde Tree, the Saguaro, and other desert species. The man, Bob, who had a magnificent obsession, with finding gold in the Superstition Mountains, was my brother-in-law. I miss our fishing trips and our search for the Lost Dutchman Mine. Although Bob is no longer with us, I will hold these adventurous moments in memory for the rest of my life.

For all my family and friends in the greater Phoenix metro area, I wish you well and hope you have some of the great, exciting, experiences I had in Arizona

★ Kelly's Perspective & Lessons Learned ★

Having lived in and loved Arizona for so many years the three things that come to mind are: family, extended family, and many friends that call this majestic state home.

Arizona is another place in the nation that can easily inspire me to write an entire book. Until then, I will share that the Valley is irresistible and the northern part of Arizona will steal your heart. When referring to the north, I would include Flagstaff, Sedona, and the surrounding areas. Northern destinations, for me, make the shortlist of things in your life that you love and can't live without.

Another shortlist item includes my husband, pictured with me while on a memorable hike in Oak Creek Canyon.

★ Famous People Born in Arizona ★

Apache Kid the Indian outlaw, born on San Carlos Apache Indian Reservation circa 1860.

Lynda Carter the actress, born in Phoenix in 1951.

Cesar Estrada Chavez the labor leader, born in Yuma in 1927.

Cochise the Apache Indian chief, born in Chiricahua country circa 1804.

Geronimo the Apache Indian chief, born near Turkey Creek in 1909.

Barry Goldwater, the politician, born in Phoenix in 1909.

Carl Trumbull Hayden the politician, born in Hayden's Ferry in 1877.

Frank Luke, Jr. the WWI fighter ace, born in Phoenix in 1897.

Linda Ronstadt the singer, born in Tucson in 1946.

Kerri Strug the gymnast, born in Tucson in 1977.

Stewart Udall the former Secretary of the Interior, born in Saint Johns in 1920.

Louie Espinoza the Arizona's first world champion boxer, born in Globe in 1962.

Michael Carbajal the world champion boxer, born in Phoenix in 1967.

Where Will You Visit?

What Photos Will You Take?

State Capital: Little Rock

State Flower: Apple Blossom

Population: 2,915,918 (Ranks 23rd, as of 2010 Census)

Land Area: 52,035.5 square miles (Ranks 27th)

Population Density: 56.0 persons per square mile (Ranks 34th)

★ Arlie's Insight & Highlights ★

Arkansas, also known as "The Natural State", is one of the prosperous states of the South. Prosperity that is driven by a combination of: agriculture, economic development, educational reform, minerals (including diamonds), natural resources and much more. Arkansas has two broad geographic features, known as the Highlands and the Lowlands. The Highlands consist of the Ozark and Boston Mountains of the north and western portion of the state. The Lowlands are found in the southern and eastern parts. It's only natural that the good and productive crop lands would be in eastern and southern Arkansas, where a variety of crops are grown. Some of the dominant crops are cotton, rice, and soybeans. Livestock and chickens are products of the highland part of the state. In northwest Arkansas, one can travel for miles and see chicken and turkey brooder houses by the dozens.

A look back in Arkansas history tells us it has been claimed by different countries in the past. It has also been claimed that De Soto of Spain may have visited the Hot Springs area as early as 1541. De La Salle, a French explorer, claimed Arkansas and all of the Mississippi Valley for France in 1682. The "Arkansas Post" is said to be the first white settlement in Arkansas. It started from a camp established in 1686, by a French explorer, Henri De Tonti.

The U.S. acquired Arkansas Territory, as part of the Louisiana Purchase, from France. Arkansas became the 25th state in the union on June 25, 1836, but Arkansas seceded from the union in 1861 and was readmitted to the Union in 1868. Arkansas fought on the side of the Confederate States during the Civil War. One of the major battles of the Civil War was fought near Rogers in Northwest Arkansas. This is known as the Battle of Pea Ridge and it is now a national military park. Union troops won an important victory there in March of 1862. Fast-forward to World War II, the birth place of General Douglas MacArthur, is located in Little Rock.

Arkansas has a multitude of places to see and things to do. We enjoy fishing the clear lakes and streams of this state. Trout is our favorite species to catch and there are several great spots for those who enjoy this sport. In the Northwest Corner is Beaker Lake found below the dam, Bull Shoals, Norfork, and Greers Ferry (all) below the dam, on the Little Red River are all super places for fishing for trout.

Cave lovers and explorers will enjoy the caves in beautiful Northern Arkansas. Civil War Cavern near Bentonville, Onyx Cave near Eureka Springs, Cosmic Cavern near Berryville, Mystic Caverns near Harrison, Hurricane River Cave near St. Joe, and Blanchard Springs Caverns, near Mountain View. Springs are another beautiful natural feature in Arkansas. Mammoth Springs is unique and one of the largest in the world. It's located at the town of Mammoth Springs near the Missouri border. When you visit the Mammoth Springs area, take along your camera, you will be glad you did when you return home.

Arkansas has many national forest areas. The Ozark National Forest in the northwestern part of the state is very large, with many hills, valleys and streams. In west-central Arkansas, one can enjoy the Ouachita National Forest. This area contains many beautiful lakes and streams, with several state parks available. Also, the highest point in the state, Magazine Mountain, is located here.

In the fall months one can take Foliage Tours in the Arkansas Mountains. The colors appear to change in the north first. The areas around Eureka Springs is a good place to start but anywhere in Northwestern Arkansas is okay. Later, the foliage is beautiful all the way south to Mena and Hot Springs National Park.

Arkansas is the only U.S. state to have a diamond mine, which is The Crater of Diamonds State Park, near Murfreesboro. Worth noting, it is the only diamond mine where the public can mine for diamonds and keep what they find. To mine for diamonds, one starts with a bucket of loose dirt and sifts it out at the water station. The largest diamond found there, in 1924, was the "Uncle Sam" diamond. It was 40.23 carats and was worth $250,000. In 1956, a white diamond was found that was 15.33 carats, and was worth a small fortune. More than 19,000 diamonds have been found here.

Kelly's Perspective & Lessons Learned

After reading this, I want to return to Arkansas and visit the Crater of Diamonds State Park.

Famous People Born in Arkansas

G. M. (Bronco Billy) Anderson the actor, born in Pine Bluff in 1880.

Maya Angelou the author and poet, born in Saint Louis in 1928.

Helen Gurley Brown the editor, born in Green Forest in 1922.

Glen Campbell the singer, born in Delight in 1936.

Johnny Cash the singer, born in Kingsland in 1932.

Jay Hanna (Dizzy) Dean the baseball player, born in Lucas in 1910.

John Gould Fletcher the poet, born in Little Rock in 1886.

John Grisham the author, born in Jonesboro in 1955.

John H. Johnson the publisher, born in Arkansas City in 1918.

Alan Ladd the actor, born in Hot Springs in 1913.

Douglas MacArthur the 5-star general, born in Little Rock in 1880.

Dick Powell the actor, born in Mountain View in 1904.

Edward Durrell Stone the architect, born in Fayetteville in 1902.

★ Where Will You Visit? ★

_____

_____

_____

_____

★ What Photos Will You Take? ★

_____

_____

_____

_____

State Capital: Sacramento

State Flower: Golden Poppy

Population: 37,253,956 (Ranks 1st, as of 2010 Census)

Land Area: 155,779.2 square miles (Ranks 3rd)

Population Density: 239.1 persons per square mile (Ranks 11th)

Arlie's Insight & Highlights

After many excursions to the state of California, we realized that this could never have been enjoyed fully on a one-visit trip. In fact, two of our visits to this state were very much extended; a combined recap follows.

We entered California from the north end, from the state of

Oregon. The first site we enjoyed was the Redwood National Park, near the coast. Looking up at those trees was so inspiring; hundreds of years of growth that has survived and thrived. Then we went south, to the city of Eureka. We never experienced anything like this in all our travels. The city of Eureka, which has hundreds of significant Victorian homes (including the nationally recognized Carson Mansion) is a state historic landmark.

The next leg of our visit was east to the Mount Shasta Whiskeytown Area, near the town of Redding. Lake Shasta Caverns and the Whiskeytown Trinity National Recreation area are here. As we went east of Redding there is a nice surprise when you visit Lassen Volcanic National Park. We encountered some workers sliding down a snowy slope on their work shovels!

From Lassen, we enjoyed the drive through scenic mountain country side on our way to the Lake Tahoe area. This area has something to offer almost any traveler, including gaming. On the way west, you must stop at the Capitol of this great state, and enjoy Sacramento.

Heading west from Sacramento, the traveler will find Napa and Santa Rosa, the area of many vineyards. I visited here many years earlier, when I had relatives in Napa and Santa Rosa.

In the San Francisco and Oakland Area, note there are many tours of the cities in the Bay Area. The old prison on Alcatraz Island is a site to see. The Golden Gate Bridge is still fascinating to all who travel to California.

California covers a very large area, about 800 miles north-to-south and 375 miles wide east-to-west. If you enter the state from the south, at San Diego or Tijuana, Mexico, you may choose to follow Highway No. 1, which follows the coastline all the way to Northern California. This is probably one of the longest scenic routes in all the U.S.

After visiting San Diego, which includes the greatest zoo in the world that is home to over 3,700 rare and endangered animals across a 100-acre footprint, we headed north to the Los Angeles area. This place is almost indescribable because of all it has to offer, including a great Hollywood tour. Traveling north on Highway No. 1, one may encounter some of the Old Franciscan Missions that started near San Diego in the late 1700s. About 20-21 of these old Missions run all the way to north of San Francisco.

One of the most famous places that we could not miss was San Juan Capistrano. We also visited the Hearst Castle near San Luis Obispo. Traveling north along the coast is the Monterey Peninsula, where one will find the beautiful small cities of Carmel, Pebble Beach, Pacific Grove and Monterey.

As we go in search of most of California's National Parks and National Monuments, we must skip to the east side of the state. Yosemite National Park is approximately 200 miles east of San Francisco Bay Area. Bridalveil Fall is majestic! One can see deer all over this park. Proceeding south, from Yosemite, we find Kings Canyon National Park and close by is Sequoia National Park. The visitor must explore this entire area to get the full pleasure of this unique place.

Mount Whitney is nearby; at 14,494 feet, this is the highest mountain in the contiguous 48 states, and is in close proximity to Death Valley, which is the lowest point. Death Valley National Park is very hot and dry, it is the total opposite of the state's high country and has the record for the hottest temperature recorded in the country. The visit must include Scotty's Castle that is built Spanish-style, by Mr. Scott, who lived in the area for more than 30 years.

Farther south is the Joshua Tree National Park. Although drought and extreme heat in recent years has killed off several of the older trees, it is worth visiting. Nearby is the famous Palm Springs, a beautiful oasis in the southern California desert. No matter where one resides in the U.S., you will find a visit to California memorable and potentially enchanting.

★ Kelly's Perspective & Lessons Learned ★

California will continue to be a favorite destination with memories of the 17-mile drive, misplacing keys on Pebble Beach, and remarkable evenings in San Francisco.

Looking forward, I now want to explore Eureka's charming Victorian homes and return to Sausalito's waterfront.

★ Famous People Born in California ★

Marcus Allen the football player, born in San Diego in 1960.

Shirley Temple Black the actress, ambassador, born in Santa Monica in 1928.

Julia Child the chef, television, born in Pasadena in 1912.

Joe DiMaggio the baseball player, born in Martinez in 1914.

Robert Frost the poet, born in San Francisco in 1874.

Jerry Garcia the guitarist, singer, born in San Francisco in 1942.

Jeff Gordon the car racer, born in Vallejo in 1971.

Jack London the author, born in San Francisco in 1876.

George Lucas the filmmaker, born in Modesto in 1944.

Richard M. Nixon the 37th U.S. president, born in Yorba Linda in 1913.

Robert Redford the actor, born in Santa Monica in 1936.

Sally K. Ride the astronaut, born in Los Angeles in 1951.

John Steinbeck the author, born in Salinas in 1902.

Serena Williams the tennis player, born in Lynwood in 1980.

Where Will You Visit?

What Photos Will You Take?

State Capital: Denver

State Flower: Rocky Mountain Columbine

Population: 5,029,196 (Ranks 22nd, as of 2010 Census)

Land Area: 103,641.9 square miles (Ranks 8th)

Population Density: 48.5 persons per square mile (Ranks 37th)

★ Arlie's Insight & Highlights ★

My dad introduced me to Colorado when I was only eight years old, so I received my Colorado Rocky Mountain High long before John Denver's hit song appeared on the Bill Board Top 40 Hits List. But the Rocky Mountains did give me a tremendous "high" at that young age and I have been under that spell until this day.

There is something magical about those big mountains that pop up out of the high plains. I imagine that the early explorers had similar feelings, when first sighting these breathtaking mountains.

My trips to Colorado when I was young were to work in the fruit orchards near Grand Junction, where we would work and then haul loads of fruit back to Oklahoma.

After growing up, my trips to Colorado were for pleasure. All the activities included hiking, climbing, camping, fishing, sightseeing, hunting and rafting. Some of the most exciting times were rafting the rapids on the rivers. We have had the privilege of rafting the upper Colorado River, the upper Arkansas River, the upper Rio Grande, and the Taylor River, which are near Almont and Gunnison.

Some of Colorado's rivers have all classes of water, from slow, smooth water to swift rapids, which are enough to excite the most adventurous.

Camping is one of the greatest activities for the summer visitors; we have camped over most of the western two-thirds of the state. The following areas are where we have enjoyed fishing, rafting and other activities during the summer months: Stonewall, South Forke, Creede, Pagosa Springs, and finally, Durango, where one can enjoy the history of the old "Steam Train" that traveled up to the mining town of Silverton, Colorado. Two other towns of great interest in southwest Colorado are Ouray and Telluride, which include great shopping and tourist sites.

As we move north, to central Colorado, Highway 50 is the main route through the mountains to the west. Texas Creek, where one can find the Royal Gorge Toll Bridge, is a very exciting place to visit. Going west we find Salida, a great rafting area, heading over Monarch pass to Gunnison, a thriving city near a large beautiful lake. This lake is the Blue Mesa Reservoir; it provides water recreation and good fishing for large numbers of visitors.

Further west on highway 50 we find Delta, Colorado, in the Gunnison River Valley, then on to Grand Junction, where lots of fruit crops are grown. This is a special place, because of the climate and small mesas at different elevations.

The next major road north of highway 50 that crosses the mountains to the west is I-70. Before we get to I-70, we must cover Highway 24, from Colorado Springs to Leadville. This is a great deal of beautiful real estate. As we travel west from Colorado Springs on Highway 24, we cross Wilkerson Pass, Trout Creek Pass, and wind up in the upper Arkansas River Valley, near Buena Vista, Colorado. This is one of my all-time favorite places in the state. We go north from Buena Vista, to Leadville, where the city's elevation is about 10,000 feet. The nights are very cool here, even in mid-summer.

After leaving Leadville, to the north, one winds up in Vail, Colorado. If you go west from Vail, the beautiful Beaver Creek area is special for skiing in winter, and, two other cities nearby are Glenwood Springs and Carbondale, which are great for summer camping and shopping. Also west from Leadville are two of the most famous areas for skiing in all of Colorado, Aspen Mountain Ski area and Snowmass Ski area, on Highway 82.

If you go east from Vail across Vail Pass, you encounter the cities of Dillon, Georgetown, Idaho Springs and Golden, then it's Denver and you are out of the mountain camping area. Now we skip north of Denver and pick up Highway 34 to guide us into Estes Park. This is the eastern gateway to Rocky Mountain National Park. In 1915, President Woodrow Wilson signed

legislation creating this magnificent park. One good camping area near Estes Park is Mary's Lake, just south of town. Just west of town, on Hwy 34 is the highest piece of paved road in the U.S. It's known as "Trail Ridge Road," crossing the Continental Divide at Milner Pass. The reason we remember this so well is that we were camped at Mary's Lake and wanted to go over the pass to Grand Lake. For several days the road would be closed by snow or blowing snow so we had to take the long way around which was another great experience.

Later, we felt the need to take the farthest road north in Colorado that goes west across the mountains. It was Highway 14, going to Walden. We stayed 7 days at Rustic, a small town on the Cache la Poudre River, to explore the river and lakes of this area, which include great fishing.

We moved west, to Steamboat Springs, where we had our time-share.

We have taken several treks to the far corners of Colorado to visit special sights. In the northwest corner of the state and a little off the beaten path is Dinosaur National Monument. Here one can see the pre-historic creatures, still in the original rocks. It is a fantastic lesson in geology! Dinosaur National Monument is Just off I-70, west of Grand Junction, in the Colorado National Monument, a special place in the early morning and late evening, with strange shadows, and spooky-looking structures of nature.

Over on Highway 50, between Delta and Gunnison, one can witness one of the deepest canyons of nature: the Black Canyon of the Gunnison National Park. The visitor is not likely to forget this place. In southwest Colorado, near Cortez, is the Mesa Verde National Park. We have had three visits to this place and each has been as thrilling as the last.

Just off Highway 160 near Fort Garland, is Great Sand Dunes National Monument , which is a great family place to visit. Children and grownups can enjoy the sand and water at the same time. Every family that journeys to this part of Colorado with grandchildren must stop to enjoy this sand and water haven. There is a special place to shower off after this experience and everyone goes home happy.

Colorado has two special places that make one feel as if he or she is going back in time: The Durango Silverton Narrow Gauge Rail Road, from Durango to Silverton and the Cumbres and Toltec Scenic Railroad from Antonito, Colorado to Chama, New Mexico. I can certainly recommend both of these trips, since I have enjoyed each trip three times and can't wait to go again.

Colorado appears to care for the wild animals and birds very well. One of the best locations to view any of the species is in Rocky Mountain National Park. Outside of the park the elk are plentiful. Just go to the Estes Park Golf Course and see how gentle they are most of the time, a real rare sight to see for wild elk.

Colorado fisheries are one of the greatest attractions for the state's tourism. People come from all over the plains to fish for Rainbow Trout and other species, found in the cold lakes and streams. Fishing the high lakes and streams has been my favorite sport for many years. As I write these lines, I can see on my wall a record Rainbow Trout caught in the late 90s that weighed 12 lbs. 8 oz.

We have enjoyed the ski lift areas in our summer months, for tourists, these are the great sightseeing trips. We understand that Colorado attracts many skiers to the world famous ski areas that are household names such as Aspen, Snowmass, Beaver Creek, Vail, Copper Mountain, Keystone, Breckenridge, Steamboat, Wolf Creek, Winter Park, and Purgatory.

Colorado is unique in one respect to summer vacations. Several spots have the capacity for a total vacation in one local area. Some of the locations are: South Fork-Creede, Durango, Gunnison, Colorado Springs-Pikes Peak, and one of my favorites, Buena Vista. I must hold the Buena Vista area close to my all-time favorite because this area is so versatile. When Buena Vista is the home base for a summer vacation, it is easy to visit Leadville and the nightly shows and other entertainment only 35 miles to the north as well as Salida with world class rafting only 25 miles to the south. For those who like fishing, there is river access to the upper Arkansas, 30 miles up or down from Buena Vista, in many places. Lake fishing is excellent within 25 miles or less to the west, southwest, and northwest. Some lake waters I know from experience are Cottonwood Lake, Chalk Lake, Wrights Lake, Crystal Lake, Clear Creek Lake, Twin Lakes and Rainbow Lake (privately held). There are more than a dozen mountain lakes that require 4 wheel drive or a hike in to go fishing.

Colorado has 54 mountain peaks above 14,000 feet and more than half of those peaks are within 50 miles of Buena Vista. If it's biking, hiking or scenic drives one is looking for, Buena Vista and the Collegiate Peaks area tops my list. Just west of town is Cotton Wood pass at 12,000 feet plus and to the north, Independence Pass at 12,095 ft. This is High Country!

Each Labor Day weekend, Buena Vista's Optimist Club and Trout Unlimited has a special Trout Derby for children up to 12 years of age. This is where my wife and I help the children, keep reels working and lines untangled. The pleasure and joy that comes from helping a child catch a trout, possibly their first, is an immeasurable experience.

Another great one stop and stay is the South Fork, Colorado area. One special place in this area is a place known as Fun Valley Resort. Many folks come here in June and stay until it closes in September. They offer about anything a vacationer could desire. They have good fishing, horseback riding, restaurants, laundry, grocery store, gas station, golf in the local area, and much more. This area has good lake and river fishing in the Rio Grande and South Fork of the Rio Grande River. This is the area where I caught my largest rainbow trout ever and thanks to my wife for netting it or I might still be crying for its loss.

No Colorado experience would be complete without seeing Denver and its surroundings. My favorite place is the Denver Museum of Natural History. I spent the better part of two days taking photos of the great display of animals and birds. The museum also has great displays of rocks and minerals.

Denver has some other special memories for me.

When I was a senior in college, I was studying urban geography. Each student had to choose an American city and make an extended oral report, with many details. I chose Denver for my report. Our text title was *The American City* by Raymond E. Murphy. I knew more detail would be needed for this report, so I corresponded with the Denver Chamber of Commerce. I received loads of information on Denver from the city officials. I used the material, gave my report, and received an A for the course. So to the City of Denver Chamber of Commerce, I say "thank you".

One last but important thought is, the advantage of vacationing in the same location each year is the many friends you make along the way. To all those friends and acquaintances, we wish you well.

Kelly's Perspective & Lessons Learned

Having traveled to Colorado over my lifetime, it is comforting that many of our family and extended family now call this state home. More important reasons to visit: Golden, Elizabeth, and Louisville.

Famous People Born in Colorado

Tim Allen the actor, born in Denver in 1953.

Zachery Ty Bryan the actor, born in Aurora in 1981.

M. Scott Carpenter the astronaut, born in Boulder in 1925.

Lon Chaney the actor, born in Colorado Springs in 1883.

William Harrison (Jack) Dempsey the boxer, born in Manassa in 1895.

Ralph Edwards the entertainer, born in Merino in 1913.

Douglas Fairbanks the actor, born in Denver in 1883.

Eugene Fodor the violinist, born in Denver in 1950.

Gene Fowler the writer, born in Denver in 1890.

Ruth Handler the toy maker, born in Denver in 1916.

Homer Lea the soldier, writer, born in Denver in 1876.

Ted Mack the TV host, born in Greeley in 1904.

★ Where Will You Visit? ★

_____
_____
_____
_____

★ What Photos Will You Take? ★

_____
_____
_____
_____

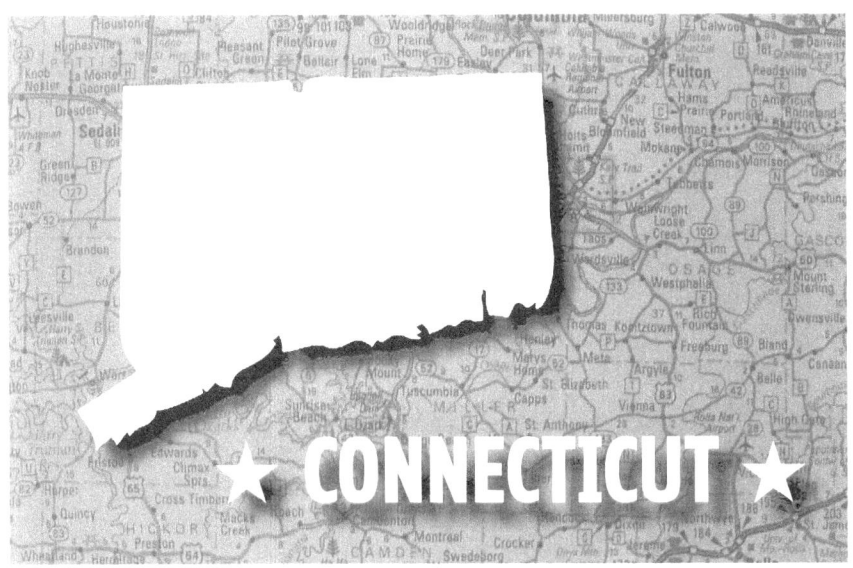

State Capital: Hartford

State Flower: Mountain Laurel

Population: 3,574,097 (Ranks 29th, as of 2010 Census)

Land Area: 4,842.4 square miles (Ranks 48th)

Population Density: 738.1 persons per square mile (Ranks 4th)

Arlie's Insight & Highlights

Connecticut, also known as the Constitution State, earned this nickname during the convention of 1787, when it broke an important deadlock over how many men should be elected from each state to the U.S. Congress. Connecticut was vital during the Revolutionary War in supplying the troops with necessary provisions to fight the war. For this, George Washington gave the state another nickname as the "Provision State".

Another important event for this state's early history was the Fundamental Orders adopted in 1639. The laws in general set forth the idea of government by consent of the people. Settlers are said to have hid Connecticut's charter in an oak tree from the English governor in 1687 in order to protect their freedom. Yale University was founded in 1701 in New Haven, making it one of the earliest institutions of higher learning in the United States. Eli Whitney was the first in manufacturing to use standard parts to make firearms. Much later, in 1954, the Atomic Submarine was launched in Groton, CT. Hartford got an early start in the insurance industry and was known in the 1800's as a reliable place for those needing insurance.

The geographical features of Connecticut are similar to other parts of New England. With the eastern upland, east of the Connecticut River, the Connecticut Valley lowlands through the center part of the state, the western uplands and the coastal lowlands and all along the Atlantic coast which include many good harbors. There are several also good beach areas in Southeast Connecticut, around Lyme and Pleasure Beach.

The rural areas and small towns contrast sharply with the industrial cities. In rural Connecticut one can see the typical New England Village of a beautiful church, a town meeting hall, a tavern and several colonial houses, either Cape Cods or other styles. It is the typical beautiful New England setting seen in books and magazines. Almost every town in the state has one or more examples of colonial architecture. Whitfield House, in Guilford, is the oldest house in the state. It was started in 1639 and is made of stone. History buffs will remember this is only 19 years after the landing at Plymouth in Massachusetts. Connecticut was one of the fastest-growing areas of New England due to great leadership and innovation.

Kelly's Perspective & Lessons Learned

Revolutionary views, intelligent colleagues, and charming towns are the first things that come to mind when I think of Connecticut. Many good memories surround the months spent near the shoreline of the state while working on a merger and acquisition.

Famous People Born in Connecticut

Ethan Allen the American Revolutionary soldier, born in Litchfield in 1738.

Benedict Arnold the American Revolutionary general, born in Norwich in 1741.

P. T. Barnum the showman, born in Bethel in 1810.

Henry Ward Beecher the clergyman, born in Litchfield in 1813.

John Brown the abolitionist, born in Torrington in 1800.

Samuel Colt the inventor, born in Hartford in 1814.

Charles Goodyear the inventor, born in New Haven in 1800.

Nathan Hale the American Revolutionary officer, born in Coventry in 1755.

Katharine Hepburn the actress, born in Hartford in 1907.

Charles Ives the composer, born in Danbury in 1874.

Annie Leibovitz the photographer, born in Waterbury in 1949.

John Pierpont Morgan the financier, born in Hartford in 1837.

Benjamin Spock the pediatrician, born in New Haven in 1903.

Harriet Beecher Stowe the author, born in Litchfield in 1811.

Noah Webster the lexicographer, born in West Hartford in 1758.

★ Where Will You Visit? ★

_____
_____
_____
_____

★ What Photos Will You Take? ★

_____
_____
_____
_____

State Capital: Dover

State Flower: Peach Blossom

Population: 897,934 (Ranks 45th, as of 2010 Census)

Land Area: 1,948.5 square miles (Ranks 49th)

Population Density: 460.8 persons per square mile (Ranks 6th)

Arlie's Insight & Highlights

Delaware is known as the "First State" because in December of 1787 it was the first state to approve the United States Constitution. Prior to this, Caesar Rodney rode 80 miles from Dover to Philadelphia to break a tie vote that allowed Delaware to approve the Declaration of Independence in the year 1776. In 1777 the British invaded northern Delaware and won a battle at a place known as Coochs Bridge. This battle was the only one fought during the Revolutionary War on Delaware soil.

In 1610, a ship under the command of Lord De La Warr, then-Governor of Virginia, sailed into Delaware Bay, and the state was given the name Delaware. Swedish Colonists founded a colony at New Sweden, the first permanent settlement, at present-day Wilmington in 1638. The Dutch then captured New Sweden in 1655, only to be taken over by the English on the Delaware River in 1664. As a result, the area was under the influence of different nations in a relatively short period of time.

Delaware fought on the side of the union during the Civil War. In 1863, President Lincoln issued the Emancipation Proclamation, freeing the slaves in all of the Confederate states in rebellion. But the act did not affect slave states that had remained loyal to the union. The slaves left in Delaware were not freed until 1865, when the United States abolished all slavery with the 13th amendment to the Constitution.

Delaware is the second smallest state in the union and more than ninety percent of its area is in the Atlantic Coastal Plains.

The state shares the area known as the Delmarva Peninsula which is also part of Maryland and Virginia, and includes great farming areas. The extreme north end of the state is considered Piedmont soil, which is a type of rocky clay, and not great for crops. Some of Delaware's leading crops are soybeans, corn, wheat, and barley. Other garden crops are beans, cantaloupes, peas, potatoes, tomatoes, and watermelon. Dairy products, poultry, and beef cattle are also found throughout the state. One product known the world over is nylon, which was first introduced to the public in 1938 by research chemists at the Du Pont Laboratories.

Delaware's laws are unique in some respects. Some of the largest corporations in America have their home offices in Delaware because state law allows companies to incorporate there

even if they do most of their business elsewhere. The reason is that it is easier and less expensive.

Things to see in Delaware: Amstel House in New Castle, the home of the New Castle Historical Society built in the 1700s, Hagley Museum Historic Site, near Wilmington, the Wilson-Warner House in Odessa and the John Dickinson Mansion, near Dover.

The entire eastern shore line is either on the Delaware Bay or the Atlantic Ocean and there are a number of beaches for recreation. The state also has many rivers. Dover, the state capital, is unique in that it is a small city with all the state leadership in one small area. Many of them spend time at the same restaurants and other establishments. We were duly impressed when we were introduced to many of the state leaders at breakfast time.

★ Famous People Born in Deleware ★

Valerie Bertinelli the actress, born in Wilmington in 1960.

Robert Montgomery Bird the playwright, author, born in New Castle in 1806.

Henry S. Canby the editor, author Seidel, born in Wilmington in 1878.

Annie Jump Cannon the astronomer, born in Dover in 1863.

Henry Heimlich the surgeon, inventor, born in Wilmington in 1920.

Ryan Phillippe, the actor, born in New Castle in 1974.

Howard Pyle the artist, author, born in Wilmington in 1853.

Where Will You Visit?

What Photos Will You Take?

State Capital: Tallahassee

State Flower: Orange Blossom

Population: 18,801,310 (Ranks 4th, as of 2010 Census)

Land Area: 53,624.8 square miles (Ranks 26th)

Population Density: 350.6 persons per square mile (Ranks 8th)

★ Arlie's Insight & Highlights ★

Florida, the Sunshine State, is named for its many days of the year with this southern exposure to the sun. This southern exposure and the many beaches make this state an ideal spot for winter vacations.

Florida is one large peninsula that protrudes into the Atlantic Ocean, and has a great coastline on the west to the Gulf of Mexico. Florida, like many states on the east coast of the United States, was very vulnerable to take over from different countries of Western Europe during its early history. Ponce de Leon claimed the region of Florida for Spain in 1513. In 1565, Spain established St. Augustine as the first permanent white settlement in what we now know as Florida. England got control of Florida in 1763, but it was ceded back to Spain in 1783. The U.S. first obtained the state of Florida from Spain in 1819 and then in 1822, Congress established the territory of Florida. A few years before the Civil War, in 1845, Florida became a state, but statehood was short-lived, because Florida joined the confederacy in 1861. After the civil war, Florida was readmitted to the union in 1868.

Florida has three main geographic regions and each one covers approximately the same amount of area. The gulf coastal plains cover most of southwest Florida and much of the Florida panhandle. The Atlantic coastal plains cover all of the eastern side of the state from Jacksonville to Miami and Homestead, which is approximately four hundred miles.

The third land region of Florida is the Florida uplands. This area consists of a large part of central Florida from Lakeland, north to the Georgia border and the northern part of the Florida panhandle. The highest point in the state is 345 ft in the panhandle, near Crestview.

Florida has many beautiful springs and a myriad of beaches that accommodate millions of visitors annually. Tourism is Florida's main industry. The Atlantic Coast appears to be the busiest, but the entire state is very attractive. Jacksonville is the largest city, but Miami is the largest metro area. In southern Florida, it's the Big Cypress Swamp and the Everglades that stand out and cover most of the land area.

Florida is the only place in the U.S. that one can find this large of a swamp-marshy environment. Another one-of-a-kind environment is found in the Florida Keys. From Key Largo to Key West is more than one hundred miles. This is one of the most exciting trips one can encounter anywhere in the United States. Be sure to take one of the boat trips out of Key West into the Gulf of Mexico and the Atlantic Ocean,

Back on mainland Florida is one of my favorite areas in the state. Mainland in Florida is defined as the land from Marco Island, north to Ft. Myers. As part of this journey, the visit to Marco Island was very special, as the beaches, views, and hotels were superb. Our next stop was in Ft. Myers to visit a friend and tour Thomas Edison's winter laboratory. It appears that Edison and Henry Ford worked together on several science projects. As we progressed north up Florida's west coast, we stayed in the Tampa and St. Petersburg area for a time. The stay on Treasure Island was beautiful and the sunsets over the Gulf of Mexico were breathtaking. Don't miss a trip to the Busch Gardens while in Tampa; it's fascinating with all the different species of birds and animals. The park provides transportation within. As one leaves the Tampa Bay area up the west coast, there are many things to see and do along this coastline all the way to Pensacola. Some memorable spots were the beaches at Panama City and the sand at Fort Walton beaches.

The state of Florida has many springs over most of the state, but two stand out. Wakulla Springs, just south of Tallahassee, is very deep and is in a beautiful setting. The other spring is near Ocala, it's called Silver Springs and it offers one of the best down-river trips one will find anywhere. Walt Disney World, near Orlando, is one of the greatest amusement parks in the world. It is a recreational center that has a Storybook Castle, submarine rides, and many different culture centers. Sea

World is also a great experience; it has a porpoise and a killer whale show and water sports special.

The area around Lakeland and Winter Haven is in a beautiful area in central Florida. The Cypress Gardens, near the town of Winter Haven has tropical gardens, water shows and it is a special attraction in the center of the state.

South of Miami, at Homestead, one can see many beautiful garden crops, and it is also very near the Everglades Park area. There is much to see and do in this area. The Shark Valley Visitors Center is on Hwy 41, on the edge of the Everglades, the Hialeah Gardens and the famous race track is nearby. As one continues north for about eight miles on I-95, it appears to be one solid city from Miami to West Palm Beach.

We also visited Cape Canaveral and the Kennedy Space Center. On arrival at the space center, we were awed by the size of the overall operation, past and present. The history at the Cape was inspiring; it covers most of what we have seen on television in years past such as the Apollo programs and the great liftoff of July 16, 1969 to start the first moon landing. The movies on some past space flights were amazing. Our main destination after leaving Cape Canaveral was to visit the historic city of St. Augustine. We wanted to see the oldest city in our country. A Spanish Explorer, Pedro de Aviles, founded the settlement in 1565. One other special interest was the mystical "Fountain of Youth", the one that Juan Ponce de Leon searched for after landing on the coast near St. Augustine in 1513. The waters of this legendary fountain were supposed to restore youth. We also visited the old moated fort, Castillo de San Marcos, it was started by the Spanish in 1672. This structure is different than other early forts in the U.S.; which was mortared construction rather than wood. A third site to visit was the oldest house in St. Augustine,

We had a personal reason for this special visit. Our relatives, a sister-in-law and husband, had inherited some real estate, just outside St. Augustine.

The inherited real estate consisted of eight lots on a plat map. My promise to our relatives before this Florida trip was to find and inspect the properties, including taking some pictures. A search at the courthouse revealed the lot numbers: 21-22-23-24-25-26-27-28. The courthouse also helped me locate the property, where I did photograph the lots. I had a plan from the start of this trip. My camera is always with me so I had collected seven great alligator photos from Wakulla Spring, Silver Springs, and Busch Gardens. All photos were great gator photos that appeared to be in their wild, natural habitat. Back home, I assembled eight photos for my sister-in-law that represented their eight lots at St. Augustine. I had alligators on lots 21-27 and a sand bar photo for Lot #28. This presentation was under a nice plastic cover when presented to them. The silence was long and facial expressions unbelievable. We let the drama play out and after they regained their composure, we showed the photos of the actual lots. My sister-in-law told me later she has shared the gator photos to all her friends and acquaintances in Wichita, Kansas.

In Florida, I was like a kid at Christmas with all the things to see and do!

Kelly's Perspective & Lessons Learned

Two words: Disney World

Famous People Born in Florida

Julian Cannonball Adderley the jazz saxophonist, born in Tampa in 1928.

Pat Boone the singer, born in Jacksonville in 1934.

Fernando Bujones the ballet dancer, born in Miami in 1955.

Fay Dunaway the actress, born in Bascom in 1941.

Dwight Gooden the baseball player, born in Tampa in 1964.

James Weldon Johnson the author, educator, born in Jacksonville in 1871.

Jim Morrison the singer, born in Melbourne in 1943.

Sidney Poitier the actor, born in Miami in 1927.

Janet Reno the attorney general, born in Miami in 1938.

David Robinson the basketball player, born in Key West in 1965.

Norman E. Thagard the astronaut, born in Marianna in 1943.

★ Where Will You Visit? ★

★ What Photos Will You Take? ★

State Capital: Atlanta

State Flower: Cherokee Rose

Population: 9,687,653 (Ranks 9th, as of 2010 Census)

Land Area: 57,513.5 square miles (Ranks 21st)

Population Density: 168.4 persons per square mile (Ranks 18th)

Arlie's Insight & Highlights

Georgia is ranked as the largest state east of the Mississippi River. The state has some coastline to the Atlantic Ocean, giving it good access to shipping some of its many products to the international marker but most of its products are consumed here in the U.S.

The earliest known European to explore what we know as Georgia, was Hernando de Soto in 1540. Much later King George II of England granted a charter to establish a Georgia colony in 1732. An Englishman, James Oglethorpe, arrived in 1733 with the first English settlers, and by 1754 Georgia became a British Royal Province. Georgia's farmers prospered but they became restless with a desire for independence similar to the one that was growing in the northern Atlantic colonies. The Revolutionary War began in Massachusetts in 1775 and several Georgians joined the movement for freedom. Some of the first battles between Georgians and the British began in the Savannah area in 1776. On July 1778, Georgia approved the Articles of Confederation, the early attempts of a U.S. Constitution. After the Revolutionary War ended in 1783, Georgia became the fourth state to ratify the United States Constitution.

During the Civil War era, Georgia fought with the Confederate States. The state's economy was based on cotton production and plantation owners believed that cotton required slave labor. In 1860 the new president was Abraham Lincoln, who was against slavery. At this time Georgia's Governor Brown led the movement for Georgia's secession from the union.

Georgia was the fifth southern state to leave the union. At the beginning of the Civil War, the Union navy was successful in closing the port of Savannah, but later many battles were to be fought on Georgia soil and many were won by Confederate forces. However, later in the war the Union forces destroyed much of Georgia during General Sherman's march to the sea. This advance on Atlanta came from Chattanooga, Tennessee and Sherman captured Atlanta in September 1863 and burned the city during November of that same year. After the Civil War ended, Georgia was readmitted to the Union in 1868 but was kicked out in 1869 because it refused to ratify the Fifteenth Amendment to the Constitution that gave all citizens the right to vote regardless of race. The state ratified the amendment in

1870 and was readmitted to the union July 15, 1870.

The geographic regions of Georgia are many, but the Atlantic Coastal Plains dominate eastern Georgia and the East Gulf Coastal Plains dominate the southwestern part of the state. Other land forms of the state are in Northern Georgia and they are: Blue Ridge Mountains, the Piedmont Region, the Ridge and valley region and the Appalachian Plateau. Georgia has a mild climate, with short, mild winters and humid summers. Due to this climate, Georgia can produce a wide variety of agricultural crops. Some of the more famous crops are: peanuts, soybeans, tobacco, cotton and peaches. Livestock and chickens are also very important to the state and broiler production is only second to that of Arkansas.

Some important places in the state of Georgia to see include: the Sculptured Confederate Leaders on Stone Mountain, near Atlanta, the Little White House, near Warm Springs (this is where President Franklin D. Roosevelt died and the F.D.R. Museum has mementos and personal belongings). Other places to visit are: the Callaway Gardens, near Pine Mountain, Kennesaw Mountain National Battlefield Park, near Marietta, The Chickamauga National Military Park, The Ocmulgee National Monument near Macon and "Old State Capitol" near Milledgeville (this was Georgia's capital from 1807-1868). Along the Atlantic coastal area, one will find the Cumberland Island National Seashore, Jekyll Island Park, Fort Frederica National Monument and Fort King George State Historic Site.

The home place of the 39th President of the United States, Jimmy Carter, is in Plains. In southeastern Georgia we found one of the most interesting places in the state of Georgia: the Okefenokee Swamp. Here, one can explore the water trails in boats with tour guides and see gators, snakes, and other wild species in their natural habitat.

★ Kelly's Perspective & Lessons Learned ★

At this point, I can share a great deal about the international airport in Atlanta due to business travel. After reading this chapter, it is clear that exploring Georgia will be a worthwhile journey.

★ Famous People Born in Georgia ★

Jim Brown the actor, athlete, born in St. Simons Island in 1936.

James E. Carter the 39th U.S. president, born in Plains in 1924.

Ray Charles the singer, born in Albany in 1930.

Ty Cobb the baseball player, born in Narrows in 1886.

Rebecca Latimer Felton the first appointed woman U.S. senator, born in Decatur in 1835.

Lawrence Fishburne III the actor, born in Augusta in 1961.

Jasper Johns the painter, sculptor, born in Augusta in 1930.

Martin Luther King, Jr. the civil rights leader, born in Atlanta in 1929.

Gladys Knight the singer, born in Atlanta in 1944.

Juliette Gordon Low the U.S. Girl Scouts founder, born in Savannah in 1860.

Little Richard the singer, born in Macon in 1932.

Jackie Robinson the baseball player, born in Cairo in 1919.

Clarence Thomas the Supreme Court Associate Justice, born in Pin Point in 1948.

Alice Walker the author, born in Putnam County in 1944.

Where Will You Visit?

What Photos Will You Take?

State Capital: Honolulu

State Flower: Hibiscus

Population: 1,360,301 (Ranks 40th, as of 2010 Census)

Land Area: 6,422.6 square miles (Ranks 47th)

Population Density: 211.8 persons per square mile (Ranks 13th)

★ Arlie's Insight & Highlights ★

Hawaii, the Aloha State, is a multi-island paradise 2400 miles from mainland USA. Visitors to Hawaii may be met by the natives with wreaths of flowers put together like a necklace, called leis, and greeted with the term *aloha* which has several meanings including: affection, peace, compassion and mercy. Since the middle of the 19th century, it also has come to be used as an English greeting to say *goodbye* and *hello*. Another Hawaiian term is hula which is a native dance. This dance is a graceful movement of the hips and arms to the music of guitars. A look back to the early history of the Hawaiian Islands reveals that not much was known about these Islands to the outside world until Captain James Cook arrived there in 1778. Captain Cook of the British Navy landed here in January of 1778 and traded with the natives who treated him well. Cook named these islands the "Sandwich Islands" after the Earl of Sandwich, who was the Lord of the British Admiralty. Early legends about the Hawaiian Islands say that the Polynesian people moved to the islands in about 1200 A.D. from Tahiti. There appears to be considerable uncertainty about the very early settlement of the islands, but one legend has it that Polynesian settlers named the island Hawaii after their chief by a similar name, Hawaii-loa.

About the time of Captain Cook's visit, the islands were ruled by different local chiefs. One chief named Kamehameha gained control of the islands after a 10 year war that began in 1782. He captured and united most of the main islands by 1795, except Kauai and Niihau. In 1810, the ruler of Kauai and Niihau joined King Kamehameha, combining the islands under one ruler. In 1887, King Kalakaua gave exclusive rights to the US for the use of Pearl Harbor. Approximately six years later, in 1893, a revolution occurred that removed the monarch, Queen Liliuokalani, from the throne. The following year, 1894, the island people established the Republic of Hawaii and by 1898 the United States had annexed Hawaii. The next two major events for Hawaii were in 1900, when the US established Hawaii as a territory, and in 1903 when the Hawaiian leadership petitioned congress for statehood. Hawaii did not become a state until 1959 at which time it became the 50th state in the Union.

The state of Hawaii has a very complex geography. There are more than one hundred islands in the chain, however, the eight main islands are: Hawaii, Maui, Kahoolawe, Molokai, Lana,

Oahu, Kauai, and Niihau. Hawaii, known as the Big Island, has more land area than all of the other islands combined. The other standout is Oahu that has approximately eighty percent of the total population of all the islands, and most of that population lives in the capital city of Honolulu.

Because of the micro climates of Hawaii, we waited for several days to fly to the island of Kauai but were never able to make the flight because of extremely rainy and inclement conditions. Rainfall can vary on some of the islands from 10 inches in the flat areas to as much as 400 inches in the mountaintops of Kauai. Micro climates can be surprising and catch travelers unaware. One such experience for us was on Maui, when we decided to drive from our hotel to the top of Haleakala Crater, the highest point on the island (10,023 feet). We were in for a sudden surprise to see high wind and snow flurries. My wife temporarily took refuge under a stranger's coat.

Many people would not realize that snow sometimes covers the high mountains of Hawaii and Maui. The two high points on Hawaii (Big Island) are Mauna Kea (13,796 ft) and Mauna Loa (13,677 ft). The high point on Maui is Haleakala (10,023 ft).

All of our experiences on the islands were exciting, because we explored many days by driving all the way on roads to the end. Every day was a day of exploring on the islands, stopping at stores, pineapple stands, sugar cane fields and Macadamia nut stands.

In order to understand the eight main islands of Hawaii, a brief overview is needed. Niihau, sometimes known as the "Forbidden Island", is a place where one must have permission of the owner in order to visit. The island was purchased from King Kamehameha V in 1864 for $10,000 by Mrs. Sinclair. The descendants of Mrs. Sinclair still own the island and use it as a cattle ranch.

Kauai is known as the "Garden Island"; it is rich in greenery and great gardens. This island is one of the wettest spots on the planet, with over 400 inches of annual rainfall.

Oahu, also known as the "Gathering Place", has about 80% of the population of all the islands. Pearl Harbor is located on the south of the island and is the headquarters of the US Pacific Fleet. This is where the Japanese pulled a surprise attack in December of 1941 and got the U.S. into World War II.

Lanai, known as the "Pineapple Island", is owned by the Dole Corporation and the land is just one large pineapple plantation.

Molokai is also called the "Friendly Island" because of the common courtesy shown to visitors of the island. Most of the island is covered with cattle ranches, but much of it is rugged mountains. The fertile portion in the central region is where many Pineapple Plantations are located.

Molokai is the place of the famous colony for victims of leprosy. On this peninsula of Kalaupapa, is where Father Joseph De Veuster worked with the victims.

Kahoolaw is the smallest of the eight major islands and it has no population. The island is used by the US Military for a target range.

Maui is also called the "Valley Island". The name comes from two volcanic mountains with a large fertile valley between them. This valley produces lots of sugar cane and pineapple from the plantations. Maui has a large national park, known as the Haleakala Crater, which is one of the world's largest inactive volcanic craters.

Hawaii was formed by five volcanoes and Kilauea on the southeastern side is still very active. This volcano attracts thousands of visitors all year. When we visited Kilauea, we could drive up almost to its edge; that's why it's sometimes called the Drive-in Volcano. We did luaus and music at night and traveled the road by day.

In Hawaii one should rent a car wherever possible in order to visit the major sights and beaches. On Oahu: Pearl Harbor's U.S.S. Arizona Memorial, the National Memorial Cemetery of the Pacific, Sea Life Park, the Valley of the Temples and the Polynesian Cultural Center. On Kauai: the Waimea Canyon, Wailua Falls and Wailua River. On Maui: the great Haleakala National Park. On Hawaii: Hilo, the orchids-growing center, the Hawaii Volcanoes National Park, and Captain Cook's Monument, as well as traveling the roads around the island. On the big island is the "Parker Ranch" the largest ranch in Hawaii, which has been in existence for over 160 years, and certainly worth visiting. Once you have landed in Honolulu and enjoyed the land of Oahu, fly to as many of the other islands as you can; it will increase your Hawaiian experience and excitement of your visit. Remember, on the Big Island, with a little imagination, you can close your eyes and listen to that Polynesian music and know you are in paradise.

Kelly's Perspective & Lessons Learned

Kauai is the first thing that comes to mind when I hear the word 'Hawaii'. It is my favorite island for several reasons and the first place I dared to get on a zipline. If your goal is to experience remarkable beauty in nature, Kauai needs to be on your itinerary.

Famous People Born in Hawaii

Hiram Bingham II the missionary, born in Honolulu in 1831.

Tia Carrere the singer, actress, born in Honolulu in 1967.

Don Ho the entertainer, born in Honolulu in 1930.

Kaahumanu the Hawaiian queen, born in a cave near Hana, Maui circa 1768.

Duke Paoa Kahanamoku the Olympic swimmer, born in Haleakala, Honolulu in 1890.

Kamehameha I the first Hawaiian king, born in Mo'okini Heiau circa 1758.

Kamehameha V the last of the dynasty, born in Honolulu in 1830.

George Parsons Lathrop the journalist, poet, born in Honolulu in 1851.

Liliuokalani the queen, last Hawaiian monarch, born in Honolulu in 1838.

Ellison Onizuka the astronaut, born in Kealakekua in 1946.

Don Stroud the actor, born in Honolulu in 1943.

★ Where Will You Visit? ★

_____
_____
_____
_____

★ What Photos Will You Take? ★

_____
_____
_____
_____

State Capital: Boise

State Flower: Syringa

Population: 1,567,582 (Ranks 39th, as of 2010 Census)

Land Area: 82,643.12 square miles (Ranks 11th)

Population Density: 19.0 persons per square mile (Ranks 44th)

★ Arlie's Insight & Highlights ★

Idaho was observed by the white men of the Lewis and Clark expedition in 1805 as they crossed the mighty Bitterroot Range and went down the Clearwater River to what is now Lewiston, Idaho. This is where the Clearwater River junctions with the

Snake River. Before this time Idaho was wild and belonged to the Native American Indians of this area. The Lewis and Clark Expedition was on their way to the Pacific Ocean by way of the Snake River and on down the Columbia River to their final destination.

Other bits of Idaho's early history come from several sources. In 1809, a Canadian explorer named David Thompson started a trading post near Lake Pend Oreille in what we know as the Idaho Panhandle. Approximately twenty-five years later, Fort Boise and Fort Hall were built. The first white settlement in the Idaho region was done by missionaries Henry Spalding and his wife, near what is now Lewiston, in 1836. By 1855, members of the Church of Jesus Christ of Latter Day Saints began farming in eastern Idaho but were run out by Indians. However, five years later, the LDS founded a permanent settlement at Franklin, in 1860.

The U.S. Congress established the Idaho Territory in 1863 and in 1864 Boise became the capital of Idaho Territory. The 1870s were a scene of trouble in Idaho. The wars with the Native Americans, came from pressure from the settlers and the U.S. Army as they tried to force the Nez Perce Indians to move from Oregon to a reservation in Idaho.

The Nez Perce Indians, led by Chief Joseph, resisted the move to a reservation and in June of 1877 they won a battle in north-central Idaho. However, the Nez Perce were soon forced to surrender near the Canadian border in October 1877 because of a larger force of the U.S. Army.

The Bannock Indians also rebelled because of a food shortage on their reservation and they had lost their hunting ground. The Bannock Indians under Chief Buffalo Horn lost in a battle with U.S. troops and their chief was killed, so the Bannock lost their spirit to continue fighting.

The geography of Idaho is split into two basic land forms: the Rocky Mountains and the Snake River Plains, which are also known as the Eastern Columbia Plateau. Most of the agriculture is in the Snake River Valley where a variety of crops are grown. The irrigation has turned the land into large fields of potatoes, sugar beets, and other crops. The state also has a great timber industry and many national forests in the northern half of the state.

Most of my personal experience has been in northern Idaho. I had the privilege of working in the National Forest Service in Libby and Troy, Montana. There were times when we spent the weekends across the border in Idaho towns that I remember well. Bonners Ferry, Sandpoint, and Coeur d'Alene were the close ones. Many years later I went bear hunting on the Montana-Idaho border east of Bonners Ferry and northwest of Troy, Montana.

Idaho has much to offer the adventurous outdoor person. Hunting, fishing, and skiing are some of the many activities one can enjoy in the state. The photo of my wife catching trout, near Montpelier, was just one example of the excitement of catching a rainbow trout in Idaho.

The ski areas are spread over much of the state: Bogus Basin Ski Area, near Boise; Magic Mountain Ski Area, near Twin Falls; Pomerelle Mountain Ski Area, near Burley; Schweitzer Mountain Ski Resort, near Sandpoint in the north and the greatest one of all, Sun Valley Ski area, near Ketchum, is well known nationally.

There are many things to see and do while traveling in Idaho. The falls on the Snake River in the southern part is a great tourist site. Shoshone Falls and Swan Falls are not far off from I-84. Other sites in the area are Craters of the Moon National Monument, Shonshone Ice Caves, and Hagerman Fossil Beds National Monument. In northern Idaho one will find: Thompson's Trading Post of 1809, Nez Perce National Historic Park and Nez Perce National Park east site.

Idaho, the smallest of the Rocky Mountain States, is a beautiful experience from one end to the other. This is why in my lens, it is a Gem State.

★ Famous People Born in Idaho ★

T. H. Bell the educator, born in Lava Hot Springs in 1921.

Gutzon Borglum the Mt. Rushmore sculptor, born in St. Charles in 1867.

Carol R. Brink the author, born in Moscow in 1895.

Frank F. Church the senator, born in Boise in 1924.

Vardis Fisher the author, born in Annis in 1895.

Harmon Killebrew the baseball player, born in Payette in 1936.

Ezra Pound the poet, born in Hailey in 1885.

Picabo Street the skier, born in Triumph in 1971.

Lana Turner the actress, born in Wallace in 1921.

★ Where Will You Visit? ★

_____
_____
_____
_____

★ What Photos Will You Take? ★

_____
_____
_____
_____

State Capital: Springfield

State Flower: Native Violet

Population: 12,830,632 (Ranks 5th, as of 2010 Census)

Land Area: 55,518.9 square miles (Ranks 24th)

Population Density: 231.1 persons per square mile (Ranks 12th)

★ Arlie's Insight & Highlights ★

Illinois, also known as the "Land of Lincoln", is the most populated of the Midwestern states. Approximately fifty years after the landing of the Mayflower at Plymouth, Massachusetts, two French explorers, Louis Joliet and Jacques Marquette, were the first white men in the area now known as Illinois. The French settlers that arrived after them named the area after the Indians that occupied the region. These Indians were Illiniwek (superior men), the French pronunciation turned out to be Illinois.

Some of the Indians of this region formed a tribal union that included the Cahokia, Kaskaskia, Peoria, and others that were called the "Illinois Confederacy". In 1699, some French priests founded a mission in Cahokia, said to be the oldest town in what is now Illinois. By 1717, Illinois was part of the French Colony of Louisiana. Turbulent years followed and France had to include Illinois in the territory it ceded to Britain after the French and Indian War ended in 1763. With the Revolutionary War in the eastern colonies beginning in 1775, it was not long until its effects were felt in what we know as the Midwest. The forces of George Clark captured Cahokia and Kaskaskia in 1778 and the area became a part of the United States with the treaty ending the Revolutionary War and the following year (1784) Virginia gave up its claim to the Federal government. In 1787, Congress made Illinois part of the Northwest Territory.

The French and British fought over the land that is now Illinois for several years, but the British finally won. After the Revolutionary War ended and Illinois became part of the U.S., its troubles were still unsettled until 1809, when Congress made Illinois a Territory. During 1812 Indians killed many white settlers while leaving from Fort Dearborn (now Chicago) and only six years later, 1818, Illinois became the 21st state in the union on December 3rd of that year.

The geography of Illinois is reasonably simple; it is mainly till plains and Great Lakes plains, with some small hills in the extreme southern part of the state. Most of Illinois is flat prairie

of rich farmland and it appears to go on forever when one flies over going to and from Chicago from the south and west. The farms appear as beautiful checkered patterns of multi-colored plains. Illinois is bordered on the west by the Mississippi River all the way from north to south and most of the eastern border is the Wabash and Ohio Rivers. The Illinois River is a great waterway within the state and runs from Chicago all the way to near Alton on the Mississippi River

Illinois is just one large "garden spot" in our nation and this fertile area runs from Ohio westward to Kansas and Nebraska and is sometimes called the corn belt. The chief crop is corn, but other crops of wheat, oats, barley, rye, soybeans and other grain crops are important to the state.

My personal experience in Illinois has been around the Chicago area from the big city north to Waukegan. Although I have crossed the state several times most of my activities have been centered in and around the greater Chicago area. To be more specific, I was employed by the Western Electric Corporation (AT&T) and the corporate education center was in Highland Park, Illinois. Yet, to be more specific, the Ed. Center was in the Moraine Hotel on Lake Michigan. This is where the corporation sent the new, young, managers to learn the activities of the company. We had great dinner parties and became acquainted with other management employees from across the country. We always chided the managers from the installation division on which forks to use first at the dinner table! All of our first trips to Highland Park were known as going away to "Charm School".

All the meetings at the Hotel Moraine were fun and exciting, but the work sessions were long days and extended into the night. Another unforgettable experience from the sessions at the hotel was an invitation from a local manager to his department at the Western Electric Factory, known as the Hawthorne Works, in Cicero, Illinois. I did agree on the visit and I was excited about it, because the Hawthorne Factory was older than the Oklahoma City Factory, which was my home base.

All my trips to Highland Park were memorable and the fall colors from Chicago north to the Wisconsin line are a beautiful sight. There are many must-see places in Chicago and the visitor must spend a few days to enjoy them. The Field Museum of Natural History has got to be one of the best in the world; I say this from experience in other cities and states of the U.S. and elsewhere. A trip out on Lake Michigan, day or night, should also be a part of any visit to the Chicago area.

Many other places outside Chicago are well-known historical sites that visitors would enjoy. Some of those sites are: Abraham Lincoln's home in Springfield, where Lincoln lived from 1844 to 1861; the home of Ulysses S. Grant, in Galena, has furnishings much as it was when Grant lived there. A small place called Nauvoo, founded as a Mormon community by Joseph Smith on the banks of the Mississippi River in 1839. Travelers can see the homes of Joseph Smith, Brigham Young, and Wilford Woodruff, the early founders of the Mormon Church. Another place worth a visitor's attention would be New Salem State Park, a reproduction of the town where Lincoln lived from 1831-1837. The buildings and shop are much like they were when Lincoln lived and studied there and the store and tavern of which Lincoln was part owner, near Springfield.

Many famous people who lived in Illinois and are remembered throughout history for their inventions and their accomplishments are a long list, but a few names that come to mind are: Abraham Lincoln, Stephen A. Douglas, Cyrus McCormic (the reaper), John Deer (the plow), Everett Dirksen, Charles Percy, and Ulysses S. Grant.

On our last visit to Chicago, we decided to stay downtown so we could walk and enjoy the city firsthand and also take guided tours around the greater Chicago area. We took in the museums, the art exhibits, Sears Tower, the parks and other landmarks around the city. It was the lake cruise that was a joyful experience. We decided the luncheon cruise was the best for us, because we could see the city and landscape, which was not visible on the night cruises.

The downtown experience was good, although different at times. One day we were walking past Harry Caray's and decided to go in for a visit, we were dressed in shorts and tee shirts for summer but it was a cool evening. We were eating peanuts, drinking a coke and admiring all the sports figures but the customers and servers were looking at us like we were from another planet! We did not lose much time leaving Harry Caray's that evening. The following day, we came dressed for the evening and had our second visit to Harry Caray's restaurant. We mingled with customers and staff, enjoyed ourselves for the total experience in downtown Chicago.

★ Kelly's Perspective & Lessons Learned ★

The Chicago Architecture Foundations tours and shopping on Michigan Avenue are my favorite ways to experience the windy city.

★ Famous People Born in Illinois ★

Gillian Anderson the actress, born in Chicago in 1968.

Mary Astor the actress, born in Quincy in 1906.

Arnold O. Beckman the inventor, born in Cullom in 1900.

Jack Benny the comedian, born in Chicago in 1894.

Marvin Camras the inventor, born in Chicago in 1916.

John Chancellor the TV commentator, born in Chicago in 1927.

Jimmy Connors the tennis champion, born in East St. Louis in 1952.

Cindy Crawford the model, born in DeKalb in 1966.

Miles Davis the musician, born in Alton in 1926.

James T. Farrell the author, born in Chicago in 1904.

Harrison Ford the actor, born in Chicago in 1942.

Benny Goodman the musician, born in Chicago in 1909.

Dorothy Hamill the ice skater, born in Chicago in 1956.

Ernest Hemingway the author, born in Oak Park in 1899.

Charlton Heston the actor, born in Wilmette in 1923.

William Holden the actor, born in O'Fallon in 1918.

Rock Hudson the actor, born in Winnetka in 1925.

Burl Ives the singer, born in Hunt City in 1909.

Quincy Jones the composer, born in Chicago in 1933.

Bill Murray the actor, born in Wilmette in 1950.

Bob Newhart the actor, comedian, born in Oak Park in 1929.

Richard Pryor the comedian, actor, born in Peoria in 1940.

Ronald Reagan the 40th U.S. president, actor, born in Tampico in 1911.

McLean Stevenson the actor, born in Normal in 1927.

Raquel Welch the actress, born in Chicago in 1940.

★ Where Will You Visit? ★

★ What Photos Will You Take? ★

State Capital: Indianapolis

State Flower: Peony

Population: 6,483,802 (Ranks 15th, as of 2010 Census)

Land Area: 35,826.1 square miles (Ranks 38th)

Population Density: 181.0 persons per square mile (Ranks 16th)

★ Arlie's Insight & Highlights ★

This state is known as the Hoosier State, although it may be more internationally known for the Indy 500 automobile race held each year inside of Indianapolis. Another internationally recognized destination is the University of Notre Dame, together with the Memorial Library Mosaic of Christ. Memorable areas include Gary, Indiana on Lake Michigan and greater city of Indianapolis that both spotlight much of the state's history.

Although the state of Indiana is the smallest of the Midwestern states, it is very important for industry and agriculture. Indiana is also known as the "Hoosier State" and the residents are known as Hoosiers. It is simply one of the nicknames that started in the early history of a state and it remains until today.

A brief look back in history tells us the first people to live in the land of what we now known as Indiana were Indians known as the "Mound Builders"; signs of their burial mounds are still visible today. Later, when the first white explorers came, about 1679 there were only Indians of the Miami tribe. Other tribes that had been in the area were known as Shawnee, Munsee, Delaware, and Mohicans. The pressure from white settlers forced most tribes to sell their land. They were also driven out by the military. By 1836 even the Potawatomi had sold their land to the government and the rest were taken out by military force in 1838.

In 1679, the first known white man to reach the area of Indiana was a French explorer named Robert Cavelier. About 1730-31, the French founded Vincennes, the first permanent settlement in the state. In 1763, the French had to give this region to the British in settlement after the French and Indian War. During the Revolutionary War, George Clark and his men captured Vincennes from the British in 1779. By the year 1800, Congress established the Indiana Territory. This included a vast area that covered what is now part of Indiana, Illinois, Wisconsin, Michigan, and Minnesota. Wars continued until General William Harrison defeated the Native Americans in 1811 at the battle of Tippecanoe. The victory over the Native Americans opened the territory for settlers. In 1816, Indiana became the 19th state in the union.

Several important events have occurred that impacted the nation. The Standard Oil Company built large oil refineries near Lake Michigan, the United States Steel Co. build large steelworks at Gary, Indiana and one of the great stories of success was the Studebaker brothers that began in South Bend, in 1852, building the Prairie Schooners that helped the families move westward on the famous expansion we read about in history books. The Studebaker Company built automobiles until the 1960's. In 1911, the first 500-mile Memorial Day auto race was held in Indianapolis and the top speed was about 75 miles per hour.

The geography of Indiana is simple: it is mainly tilled plains, great lake plains, and the southern hills and lowlands. The central till plains are part of the expansive corn-belt, which is great for agriculture. The sand dunes along Lake Michigan are a great place to visit. They run all the way into the state of Michigan.

Some interesting places to visit are: Lincoln's Boyhood National Memorial, which is the farm where Lincoln lived from age 7 through age 21; the William Henry Harrison Home, where Harrison lived while serving as Indiana's first territorial governor. Wyandotte Cave, one of the largest caves in the U.S., Lincoln's Pioneer Village, a memorial to Lincoln's 14 years in Indiana; and the park county covered bridges that number 30 or more.

★ Famous People Born in Indiana ★

Larry Bird the basketball player, born in West Baden in 1956.

Bill Blass the fashion designer, born in Fort Wayne in 1922.

James Dean the actor, born in Marion in 1931.

Bernard F. Gimbel the merchant, born in Vincennes in 1885.

Virgil Grissom the astronaut, born in Mitchell in 1926.

Michael Jackson the singer, born in Gary in 1958.

David Letterman the TV host, comedian, born in Indianapolis in 1947.

Shelley Long the actress, born in Fort Wayne in 1949.

John Cougar Mellencamp the singer, songwriter, born in Seymour in 1951.

Cole Porter the songwriter, born in Peru in 1891.

J. Danforth Quayle the vice president, born in Indianapolis in 1947.

Red Skelton the comedian, born in Vincennes in 1913.

Willis Van Devanter the Supreme Court justice, born in Marion in 1859.

★ Where Will You Visit? ★

_____
_____
_____
_____

★ What Photos Will You Take? ★

_____
_____
_____
_____

State Capital: Des Moines

State Flower: Wild Rose

Population: 3,046,355 (Ranks 30th, as of 2010 Census)

Land Area: 55,857.1 square miles (Ranks 23rd)

Population Density: 54.5 persons per square mile (Ranks 36th)

★ Arlie's Insight & Highlights ★

The endless fields of corn and farms that dot the Iowa landscape have a type of simple beauty that is often unappreciated. Across the Hawkeye State from end-to-end you will be awed by the lush fields of corn and picturesque farms. This state is truly the center of the U.S. bread basket as Iowa now has more than 92,000 farms, at the time of this writing and according to department of agriculture.

One of the great attractions for the people and travelers is the Iowa State Fair in Des Moines. With international acclaim, the Iowa State Fair annually attracts more than a million attendees from around the world. Recognized by *Midwest Living* magazine, *USA Weekend* and considered America's classic state fair, Iowa's ag-extravaganza is also featured in the *New York Times* best-selling travel book, *1000 Places to See Before You Die*. The book has been described as "an around-the-world, continent-by-continent listing of places guaranteed to give you the shivers."

A proud tradition since 1854, the Fair inspired the internationally-acclaimed novel, *State Fair*, three motion pictures, plus Rodgers and Hammerstein's Broadway musical. Special features include one of the world's largest livestock shows, the country's largest state fair foods department (e.g., 900 classes), the state's largest arts show, hundreds of competitive events and wacky contests; 600 plus exhibitors and concessionaires selling quality and tasty treats, and 160 rolling acres of campgrounds.

Favorite cities we visited in addition to Des Moines include Davenport on the Mississippi and Waterloo. Both of these destinations have cultural attractions, expansive parks and developed downtown districts that contribute to a community you will want to learn about.

Iowa, also known as the Hawkeye State, has an early history much like other states in the Midwest. The early settlers had trouble with the Native American Indians. This region was at one time the home of the Indians called "Mound Builders". The early explorers to this land found woodland and plains Native Americans living all across the area. The Native Americans chased after the great buffalo herds which was their main food supply. Later, the Sauk and Fox Tribes came to Iowa after the French chased them out of the Wisconsin area. This added to the many tribes already in the region, which included the Illinois, Iowa, Miami, Ottawa, and Sioux. living along the Mississippi River and other tribes occupied the western part Many years later, in 1832, a famous Native American Chief, Black Hawk, led the Sauk and Fox tribes against the whites. The Native Americans lost and they gave up much land along the Mississippi River and the permanent settlers began in the area in 1833.

As early as 1673, two Frenchmen, Louis Joliet and Jacque Marquette, were the first white men to explore this region of the Midwest. Later, in 1762, France ceded part of its Louisiana Colony, including this Iowa region, to Spain, but in 1800 Spain ceded the Louisiana Colony back to France. In 1803, the United States acquired Iowa and other areas in the Louisiana Purchase. The first U.S. fort built in the Iowa area was Fort Madison, in 1808. Permanent settlements began after the Black Hawk War ended in 1833. After settlement began, things started moving fast for this area. In 1834, Congress attached the area to Michigan for governmental purpose and in 1836, the government created the territory of Wisconsin that included Iowa, Minnesota and part of the Dakotas. Two years later, in 1838, Congress created the Iowa Territory. Eight years later, in 1846, Iowa became the 29th state in the union on December 28th.

Iowa's geography is essentially flat plains, that consists of drift plains and till plains in the northeast part of the state. The river drainage in the eastern two thirds of the state run south and east into the Mississippi River and the rivers in the western one third of the state run south and west to drain into the Missouri River.

Iowa has several places of interest for the visitor and many of them are found in the eastern part of the state: the Midwest Old Settlers and Threshers Heritage Museum, President Hoover's home at West Branch, Crystal Lake Cave, Effigy Mounds National Monument, 17 Spook Caves, and Little Brown Church in the Vale at Nashua. In the northwest is the Grotto of the Redemption.

We have traveled on I-80 from west to east and I-35 from south to north, also I-29 from Sioux City down to Missouri and Iowa has more beautiful, lush farms with traditional red barns than any of the fifty states where we have traveled.

★ Kelly's Perspective & Lessons Learned ★

Looking forward to visiting Iowa in the future, as I have colleagues and friends who enjoy living in the picturesque farm land.

★ Famous People Born in Iowa ★

Johnny Carson the TV entertainer, born in Corning in 1925.

William Buffalo Bill Cody the scout, born in Le Claire in 1846.

William Frawley the actor, born in Burlington in 1887.

George H. Gallup the poll taker, born in Jefferson in 1901.

Herbert Hoover the 31st U.S. president, born in West Branch in 1874.

Cloris Leachman the actress, born in Des Moines in 1926.

Glenn L. Martin the aviator, manufacturer, born in Macksburg in 1886.

Glenn Miller the bandleader, born in Clarinda in 1904.

Donna Reed the actress, born in Denison in 1921.

James A. Van Allen the space physicist, Mount Pleasant.

John Wayne the actor, born in Winterset in 1907.

Robert Meredith Willson the composer, born in Mason City in 1902.

Grant Wood the painter, born in Anamosa in 1891.

★ Where Will You Visit? ★

★ What Photos Will You Take? ★

State Capital: Topeka

State Flower: Sunflower

Population: 2,853,118 (Ranks 33rd, as of 2010 Census)

Land Area: 81,758.7 square miles (Ranks 13th)

Population Density: 34.9 persons per square mile (Ranks 40th)

★ Arlie's Insight & Highlights ★

The Sunflower State, sometimes known as the Midway, USA, is unique in many ways. It has seemingly endless fields of wheat and storage elevators that look like entire cities. The larger ones are in Kansas City, Hutchinson, and Wichita, but almost all smaller towns have grain elevators. Kansas leads all the states in wheat production. Kansas has also been called the "Breadbasket of America". Cities of interest for visitors would include Wichita, Kansas City, Topeka, and historic Dodge City. Wichita has air craft manufacturing like no other city you would ever visit.

A bit of early history of the state tells of a very turbulent episode that lasted for many years. One of the state's most famous towns was Dodge City, in western Kansas. Dodge City was "Trail Head" also known as the Cowboy Capital and at one time it was the largest cattle market in the world. Cowboys drove large herds of Texas Longhorns up from Texas through Oklahoma territory into Kansas to the marketplaces. This presented a challenge as it would occasionally bring trouble or unrest to the communities. Several famous lawmen such as Wyatt Earp, Wild Bill Hickok, and Bat Masterson stepped up to the challenge. Kansas does have another famous nickname, the "Jayhawks," which is still used in some of their sport teams. The people who fought to keep Kansas a free state were called Jayhawks. These violent conflicts over slavery caused the newspapers to call this the bleeding Kansas. Some of the violence lasted until after the Civil War ended in 1865.

The first white explorer to enter this land was the Spanish explorer, Coronado, his party was searching for gold but they found no treasure and departed without starting any settlements. Much later, in the 1600s, the French explorers laid claim to large areas of North America for the French, including Kansas. Then, in 1803, the U.S. purchased the territory from France in the famous "Louisiana Purchase". The Spanish still claimed parts of what would be southwest Kansas; this was later to be a part of Mexico.

Sometime between 1825 and 1842, when several Native American tribes were forced out of lands in the eastern U.S. they moved to the Kansas region. Some of the tribes included Sauk, Fox, Chippewa, Delaware, Shawnee, Kickapoo, Wyandot, Ottawa, and Potawatomi. In 1827, Colonel Henry Leavenworth

established the first permanent white settlement at Fort Leavenworth, but other whites were crossing the land after the opening of the Santa Fe Trail in 1821. Many of the Native American tribes failed to adjust to this new land. The Federal Government took back most of the land and in 1854 opened the area for white settlement. This caused the government to force many of the Native Americans to move to Oklahoma. At the same time, the plains Native Americans were fighting the settlers who were traveling across the prairie. After many years of fighting, the tribes were conquered and forced to live on reservations in Oklahoma. In 1854, the U.S. established the territory of Kansas and in 1861 Kansas became the 34th state in the union on January 29th, just before the Civil War began.

The geography of Kansas is mainly flat, with a general slope from west to east. The western part of the state is very close to the area known as the high plains, which are 4000 feet or above. The western two-thirds of Kansas is the Great Plains, the eastern one-third is Southeastern Plains and the northeastern corner is till plains, because it was glaciated during the ice age.

There are many historical places to visit in Kansas. Fort Leavenworth is where the first permanent white settlement was established in 1827. The pony express station in Hanover served as the stopover for the mail riders; this is the only station still unchanged from 1860-1861. The boyhood home of President Dwight Eisenhower also has a museum and library close by. There is also Fort Larned historic site and most interesting is "Front Street" in Dodge City that has been recreated to give it that 1870s look, which, along with the Old Cemetery and Boot Hill, reflects that famous cow-town history.

Some of our memorable times were hunting pheasant in the southwestern part of the state at Liberal, Sublette, Hugoton, and Ulysses. One week we had nice warm weather, but opening day, we had blizzard-like cold rain, so we had to run for cover. After the high winds blew tumbleweeds across the fields and into the roads, it appeared everything was moving south, so we took the hint and moved south right into Oklahoma.

★ Kelly's Perspective & Lessons Learned ★

After traveling to and through Kansas for several years, it is comforting that many of our family and extended family continue to call this state home. Important reasons to visit: Lawrence, Shawnee Mission, and Olathe.

★ Famous People Born in Kansas ★

Gwendolyn Brooks the poet, born in Topeka in 1917.

Walter P. Chrysler the auto manufacturer, born in Wamego in 1875.

Clark M. Clifford the secretary of defense, born in Fort Scott in 1906.

John Steuart Curry the painter, born in Dunavant in 1897.

Bob Dole the politician, born in Russell in 1923.

Amelia Earhart the aviator, born in Atchison in 1897.

Milton S. Eisenhower the educator, born in Abilene in 1899.

Dennis Hopper the actor, born in Dodge City in 1936.

Walter Johnson the baseball pitcher, born in Humboldt in 1887.

Stan Kenton the jazz musician, born in Wichita in 1911.

Charles Buddy Rogers the actor, born in Olathe in 1904.

Barry Sanders the football player, born in Wichita in 1968.

Vivian Vance the actress, born in Cherryvale in 1909.

★ Where Will You Visit? ★

_____

_____

_____

_____

★ What Photos Will You Take? ★

_____

_____

_____

_____

State Capital: Frankfort

State Flower: Goldenrod

Population: 4,339,367 (Ranks 26th, as of 2010 Census)

Land Area: 39,486.3 square miles (Ranks 37th)

Population Density: 109.9 persons per square mile (Ranks 22nd)

★ Arlie's Insight & Highlights ★

Kentucky is known as the state as where champion horses are raised and tobacco is grown. Kentucky got its nickname from the beautiful powdery blue grass that grows in much of the state hence, "The Bluegrass State." Although the two main products, race horses and tobacco, are very important to the state, many other products are also important. These include: beef cattle, hogs, milk, chickens, barley, oats, rye, apples and peaches. Kentucky is a well-rounded producer of useful products.

Kentucky's history had a very turbulent time from its beginning to statehood. In May 1792 the state adopted a constitution to prepare it for statehood and on June 1, 1792, Kentucky joined the union as the 15th state. Prior to statehood, much effort and skill on the frontier was required. The early white explorers found many tribes of Native Americans in the region, such as: Cherokee, Delaware, Iroquois and Shawnee. About 1750, an explorer named Thomas Walker explored the Kentucky Region, but made no settlements. As early as 1776 Daniel Boone was exploring the eastern part of the region and he returned again in 1769 to spend two years in the area known as the Bluegrass part of Kentucky. In 1773, Daniel Boone brought settlers into Kentucky, but the Native Americans forced them out. In 1774, James Harrod brought in a group of colonists from Pennsylvania and established the first permanent white settlement at Harrodsburg.

The geography of Kentucky is very complex. Beginning on

the eastern part of the state, is the Appalachian Plateau, which consists of pine mountains and plateaus. The second large area is the Bluegrass Region which contains great meadows, and horse country. The third large area in the central part of the state is Southwestern Mississippi Embayment, sometimes called the "Pennyroyal Region." In the northwestern part of the state is the western coal field and a small region of the western tip of Kentucky is known as the East Gulf Coastal Plains which has a wide flood plain with swamps and oxbow lakes.

The state of Kentucky has many interesting places to visit. Some are historic sites while others are just the natural beauty of the state. Around Lexington, the meadows and horse farms are something not found anywhere else in similar settings. There are more than 30 that are open to the public. This is where thousands of thoroughbreds are born. Elizabethtown, the location of Abraham Lincoln's father, has a museum of Lincoln's possessions as well as Native American relics. Near Bardstown is the home, built in the 1790s, that inspired Stephen Foster to write the state song, "My Old Kentucky Home." Mammoth Cave is a famous natural wonder and one that a visitor does not soon forget; in a word it is memorable. Cumberland Falls over in Southeastern Kentucky is like a mini Niagara Falls. Cumberland Gap National Historic Park is also a beautiful place.

In Central Kentucky, one can see the Perryville Battlefield State Historic site, the Constitution Square State Historic Site, the Lincoln Boyhood Home, and the Abraham Lincoln Birthplace National Historic site. The Fort Knox Gold Vault, built in 1936, is where the Federal Gold Reserve is housed.

One of my favorite places to visit was near Shakertown. There is plaque at Shakertown that states briefly the Shaker History. It reads: "Mother Ann Lee and a small band of converts came from England to New York, in 1774. She was founder of Shakerism in America. Shakerism introduced in Mercer County by Elisha Thomas, Samuel and Henry Banta. After attending a revival at Concord, Burbon Co., Kentucky, on August 15, 1805, they were converted by missionaries to acceptance of the doctrine of United Society of Believers in Christ Second Appearance. 1806-Belivers located at Shawnee Run on Thomas' Farm near each other for religious worship and protection on Dec. 3, the first family convert signed, by 44 converts, agreeing to mutual support and common-property ownership. In 1808 the first meeting house built. Name "Shaker" came from vigorous worship practice. The Shakers were devout, orderly and followed celibacy; excellent in architecture, farming and inventions. At its height there were 500 members, 5,000 acres of land with 25 miles of rock fence. In 1910, the last 12 members deeded land to private citizens, to care for them during life. In 1923 the Sister Mary Settle, the last Shaker in Mercer County, died. In 1961 the present restoration was begun."

★ Kelly's Perspective & Lessons Learned ★

Traveling in and around Kentucky was always a pleasure as I was often near the magnificent horse farms. Building on my love for horses, it makes sense that one of my favorite destinations is the Kentucky Horse Park. Background of the Park follows: in 1972, Mary Edwards sold her property to the Commonwealth of Kentucky and in 1978, the Kentucky Horse Park, the world's only park dedicated to man's relationship with the horse, opened to the public.

Today, the Park showcases over 25 live breeds in the Horses of the World Barn and covers 1,229 acres of Kentucky's famous Bluegrass. This land provides space for the park's tourist attractions, competition facilities, 260-site resort campground, and offices of more than 30 national and regional equine organizations and associations, as well as open farmland for pastures for the beloved horses in residence.

★ Famous People Born in Kentucky ★

Muhammad Ali the boxer, born in Louisville in 1942.

Louis D. Brandeis the jurist, born in Louisville in 1856.

Kit Carson the scout, born in Madison County in 1809.

George Clooney the actor, born in Lexington in 1961.

Rosemary Clooney the singer, born in Maysville in 1928.

Jefferson Davis the president of the Confederacy, born in Fairview in 1807 or 1808.

Irene Dunne the actress, born in Louisville in 1898.

David W. Griffith the film producer, born in LaGrange in 1875.

Abraham Lincoln the 16th U.S. president, born in Hodgenville in 1809.

Loretta Lynn the singer, born in Butcher Hollow in 1932.

Carry Amelia Nation the temperance leader, born in Garrard County in 1846.

Diane Sawyer the broadcast journalist, born in Glasgow in 1945.

Allen Tate the poet and critic, born in Winchester in 1899.

Hunter Thompson the writer, born in Louisville in 1937.

Robert Penn Warren the author, born in Guthrie in 1905.

★ Where Will You Visit? ★

_____
_____
_____
_____

★ What Photos Will You Take? ★

_____
_____
_____
_____

State Capital: Baton Rouge

State Flower: Magnolia

Population: 4,533,372 (Ranks 25th, as of 2010 Census)

Land Area: 43,203.9 square miles (Ranks 33rd)

Population Density: 104.9 persons per square mile (Ranks 24th)

★ Arlie's Insight & Highlights ★

Louisiana is a model of the "Old South", with many of the Antebellum homes built before the Civil War. It is common and very exciting to take a tour on the colorful paddle-wheel boats that are reminiscent of the "old days". Equally as interesting are the modern day tugboats pushing long chains of river barges up the mighty Mississippi to far reaching destinations. From a size perspective, New Orleans ranks as one of the world's busiest ports and ocean going ships can travel hundreds of miles up the river to several other popular ports.

Stepping back in time, Louisiana was named by the French explorer Robert Cavelier De La Salle, when he traveled down the Mississippi in 1682 and claimed the entire river drainage for France. La Salle named the region of Louisiana for King Louis XIV. The state has an appropriate nickname, The Pelican State, for all the brown pelicans that occupy the marshes along the coast.

From the 1760's to the 1790's, approximately 4,000 French settlers arrived in Louisiana, as they were forced out of eastern Canada by British troops. The descendants of these Canadians became known as "Cajuns". In 1699, the Royal French Colony of Louisiana was founded. In 1718, Jean Baptiste founded New Orleans. Much later, in 1762, France ceded Louisiana to Spain, and in 1800, Spain ceded Louisiana back to France. The big move came in 1803, when the United States made the Louisiana Purchase. A few years later, on April 30, 1812, Louisiana entered the union as the 18th state.

Following statehood, the U.S. was still having trouble with the British and one of the decisive battles occurred in Louisiana. In 1815, General Andrew Jackson defeated the British in the Battle of New Orleans. All progressed reasonably well until the 1850's and by 1861 Louisiana seceded from the union and joined the Confederacy, but early into the war, union troops captured New Orleans and it was not until after the war, in 1868 that Louisiana was readmitted to the union.

Geographically, Louisiana is generally flat with three major land areas, the largest area takes in more than one half of the state's footprint and it is the West Gulf Coastal Plains. The Mississippi Alluvial Plains, is a wide area that parallels the big river and the smallest land region is the East Gulf Coastal Plains.

The Mississippi Delta was formed of much silt brought down river other thousands of years. The Alluvial Plain covers about one third of the state and is home to good fertile soil. Louisiana's Tidal Shoreline, including all the bays and islands, is over 7,000 miles long. Only Alaska and Florida have longer tidal shorelines. The dominate feature of all in the state is the mighty Mississippi River, that drains about one third of the lower 48 states.

Some of my military experience in Louisiana was spent in Leesville, Fort Polk, and Lake Charles. In these popular cities, I was also introduced to the special, spicy coffee of Louisiana that includes chicory.

More recently, our trips to Louisiana were to visit some of the Antebellum homes along the Mississippi River. To put the popularity of Mardi Gras in perspective, we spent significant time and made many phone calls over a two year period to find lodging in New Orleans at the time of the annual celebration. Unfortunately, we discovered that the properties we were interested in were booked several years in advance! Learn from our experience and plan your Mardi Gras visit well in advance.

As far as popularity outside of Mardi Gras, millions of tourist visit Louisiana every year to see the French Quarters, Jackson Square and other sites around the greater New Orleans area. Other destinations in southern Louisiana that are important to see include: Avery Island, near the marshes at New Iberia; Rip Van Winkle Garden, also near New Iberia as well as Grand Island which is south of New Orleans. It has been said, of Grand Island, that some of the descendants of the Pirate, Jean Laffite still live in villages nearby. Feliciana Country is where the naturalist J.J. Audubon, made many sketches of the wild birds in the area and this location has several old plantation homes, with some open to the public. One place a visitor must see is the Chalmette National Historic Park - this is where part of the famous Battle of New Orleans was fought during the War of 1812. The site was established in 1939, in memory of Soldiers who died there. For the serious traveler, one must take a Riverboat tour to see the greatest of the Antebellum homes.

Next, I want to share two of our favorite stops located up the river from New Orleans. The first is the Nottoway Plantation House at White Castle, Louisiana. This landmark was completed in 1859 for the John Randolph family that included 11 children. The historic plantation home survived the Civil War (1861-1865) with only a minor grapeshot (e.g., a cluster of small cast-iron balls formerly used as a charge for a cannon) to one of the columns. The Nottoway originally occupied about 1,000 acres, part upland and 600 acres of swamp. The home itself was surrounded by sugarcane as well as oak trees. Construction of Nottoway included cypress logs cut and cured underwater for a total of 4 years which made the wood durable and termite resistant. Mr. Randolph would spare no expense in the construction of this home. The Nottoway was completed in 1859 at an estimated cost of $80,000 (the equivalent of $2.2 million in 2016 dollars). The design was a combination of Greek Revival and the Italianate style of architecture with an impressive 53,000 square feet of living space.

For the exterior, Mr. Randolph hired a skilled mason to complete two huge flights of granite steps for the front of the house. These steps were built with the left side intended for the ladies, with the right side for the men. The steps for the men can be identified by the boot scrapers at the bottom. The separate staircases were constructed so that men would not see the women's ankles beneath their skirts as they climbed, which was considered a severe breach of social etiquette in those days.

Interestingly, the Nottoway has 365 openings (e.g., 165 doors

and 200 windows) to the exterior, one for each day of the year. Additional interior detail reveals three floors, six staircases, 64 rooms with 26 closets together with a first floor bowling alley that has been turned into a museum and banquet area for guest at this time. Following Mr. Randolph's death, Mrs. Randolph sold the plantation in 1889 for $100,000.

Today, Nottoway has been restored and is open to guided tours, which includes the grounds and museum that tells the history of the Randolph Family as well as the plantation. Our visit included a lunch in the mansion's restaurant along with a great tour of the area. Clearly a memorable experience!

The Houmas House, also known as the Burnside Plantation and Gardens, is part of a complex that also houses a museum, located in Burnside, Louisiana. This plantation started when Alexander Latil and Maurice Conway acquired all the Houmas Tribe's land on the east side of the Mississippi River in 1774. Mr.

Latil built a French Colonial style plantation house at the site around 1775. It was originally a sugar plantation and in 1803, when the U.S. made the Louisiana Purchase from France. The Houmas was purchased later by Daniel Clark, who began to develop the property and built one of the first sugar mills in this area. In 1811, General Hampton purchased Clark's property together with his entire staff. This acquisition built on Hampton's net worth, that ranked him as one of the wealthiest landowners in the south. About 1825, the property was taken over by John Smith Preston. Mr. Preston was married to Caroline Hampton, the daughter of Wade Hampton.

The Preston's built a new main house in front of the old one in 1840. This new house was a Greek Revival Mansion, two-and-a-half stories high and surrounded by 14 large Doric columns on three sides. In 1857, this estate of 10,000 acres was sold to John Burnside, a native of Belfast, Ireland. Within a short time Mr. Burnside had built four sugar mills to process the plantation crops.

Burnside, a lifelong bachelor, died in 1881 and left the estate to a friend, Oliver Bierne. Next the property went to William Miles, Bierne's son-in-law. After the death of Mr. Miles in 1899, the property was divided up and the house was in need of much repair. In 1940, the house and what was left of the property was purchased by Dr. George Crozat, who began a great restoration program on the residence and gardens.

Fast forward, the Houmas House has been a location for a variety of movie filming, television series and commercials including: *Hush Hush Sweet Charlotte* with Bette Davis (1964), select episodes of *All My Children* (1981), *Snow Wonder* (2006) and *Wheel of Fortune* (2011).

These are only two memorable examples of what visitors will

discover in Louisiana. We highly recommend exploring Louisiana and allocating enough time to see all that this significant state has to offer.

★ Kelly's Perspective & Lessons Learned ★

Visits to the charming and bustling city of New Orleans have revolved around Aviation conferences. Although schedules were full of business meetings, I was able to escape for a few meals. A favorite dining establishment is Chef Emeril Lagasse's flagship restaurant in the New Orleans Warehouse District. You will want to consider reservations, as this fine establishment has captured culinary awards by *Esquire* and *Wine Spectator*.

★ Famous People Born in Louisiana ★

Louis Armstrong musician, born in New Orleans in 1901.

Geoffrey Beene fashion designer, born in Haynesville in 1927.

Truman Capote writer, born in New Orleans in 1924.

Fats Domino musician, born in New Orleans in 1928.

Bryant Gumbel TV newscaster, born in New Orleans in 1948.

Mahalia Jackson gospel singer, born in New Orleans in 1911.

Dorothy Lamour actress, born in New Orleans in 1914.

Jerry Lee Lewis singer, born in Ferriday in 1935.

Wynton Marsalis musician, born in New Orleans in 1961.

Jelly Roll Morton jazz musician, composer, born in New Orleans in 1890.

Cokie Roberts journalist, born in New Orleans in 1943.

Kordell Stewart football player, born in New Orleans in 1972.

★ Where Will You Visit? ★

_____

_____

_____

_____

★ What Photos Will You Take? ★

_____

_____

_____

_____

State Capital: Augusta

State Flower: White Pine Cones

Population: 1,328,361 (Ranks 41st, as of 2010 Census)

Land Area: 30,842.9 square miles (Ranks 39th)

Population Density: 43.1 persons per square mile (Ranks 38th)

★ Arlie's Insight & Highlights ★

Our two visits to Maine have been interesting and memorable at the same time. On one occasion, we witnessed a near tragedy that I will explain later. While other moments, left us surrounded by breathtaking beauty.

In our quest to see most of the National Parks across the 50 states, we discovered that the one in Maine (Acadia National

Park), which is off the beaten path, delivered a one-of-a-kind visit. Further, the many islands along the coast of Maine are surprising, it is so different than most of our east coast travels, and these islands must number in the thousands. It is easy to see why the early explorers used the term 'Main' to distinguish the mainland from the offshore islands.

The state of Maine, also known as "The Pine Tree State" is appropriately named because it is ninety-percent covered with beautiful trees. The white pine holds a special place in my memory because I worked with the white pines in western Montana when I was employed with the U.S. Forest service. Maine's trees are the raw material for a great wood processing industry, where a wide variety of goods are produced. When I studied geography in college, another important product was mentioned often: potatoes. Yes, potatoes are grown in large fields of Aroostook County where they have deep fertile soil. The fishing industry is also active and important to the state. Maine leads all the states in the amount of lobsters caught for market and almost all coastal villages have at least a small fleet of fishing boats.

It's interesting to take a brief flash back into Maine's early history. Some theories suggest the Vikings may have been visiting the coast of Maine as well as eastern Canada in the 1100's, although I don't know how concrete the history is surrounding these accounts. What is clear is that John Cabot documented his explorations of the Maine coastline around 1498. It was in 1607 that English settlers established a village at Popham near the Kennebec River; this was approximately 13 years before the Pilgrims were to land at Province Town and Plymouth, Massachusetts. A short time after the Pilgrims landed at Province Town, a royal charter was given for Maine lands and to Sir Ferdinando Gorges along with John Mason. This large tract of land was in what is now Maine and New Hampshire. This land was divided in 1629, between the two and Gorges received the portion now known as Maine. Gorges did establish a government in Maine in 1636 and five years later, in 1641, he founded the community, Gorgeana (later, York). Notably, this city was the first chartered English town in the U.S.

After Gorges died in 1647, major disputes occurred until 1664 when an English board of commissioners ordered that Maine be restored to the gorges family. The state of Massachusetts gained title to Maine in 1677, when it bought the area from the Gorges Family for $6,000. Many turbulent years followed for this region during the French and Indians Wars until the battles were ended with the treaty of Paris in 1763.

During the Revolutionary War that started in 1775, Maine sent hundreds of men to fight with the colonists' for the independence from England. In June, 1775 a group of Maine patriots captured a British ship, The Margaretta. Later, they tried to capture Quebec from the British but failed.

After the Revolutionary War ended, a movement began for separation of Maine from Massachusetts and for Maine to join the Union. This condition endured until the War of 1812, the separation movement grew much stronger and in 1819, the people voted for separation. On March 15, 1820 – Maine joined the Union as the 23rd state. However, Maine's admission to the Union became part of the Missouri Compromise. The Compromise was for Maine to join the Union as a "Free State" and Missouri to enter as a "Slave State". This was an attempt to keep the number of Slave and Free State's equal.

Switching gears, the geography of Maine is a natural and fairly simple one. The coastal lowlands follow along the Atlantic coast. The New England upland (largest in area) runs all through the central part of Maine and the White Mountains cover all the north and west part of the state, where it joins Canada and New Hampshire. The White Mountain area has many ski resorts and lakes. The coastal low lands are the location of most of the larger cities and are the most populated.

Maine has a rich history of early America lore and many sights for the visitor. Beginning at the south end of I-95, one can see; the John Paul Jones Memorial, near Kittery, the Seashore Trolley Museum, near Kennebunk, The Eagle Island state historic sight, near Baily, Ft Popham, near Popham Beach, Ft. William Henry Memorial, near Boothbay Harbor, the Montpelier Historic site, near Rockland along with many more sites near the coast. Up state Maine is beautiful all the way to New Brunswick. If you go north into Quebec, up Highway 201, Jackman will be your last stop before you go into Canada, were we once had the pleasure of staying.

Before I go rambling, I must share one of our favorite spots in all of Maine. This is "Bar Harbor" which we call the dream town of New England. I think most visitors will agree this is one heavenly place after they view the photos within this story. It is a place where one just wants to set quietly for a time to

take in the beauty and peacefulness that can be found in this memorable town. Bar Harbor also has a special ferry service to Yarmouth Nova Scotia, if you are interested in extending your journey into Canada.

Another special visit near the Bar Harbor area is the only National Park in New England; the Acadia National Park. It is different than any other park and you will have the feeling of being surrounded by water – and you will be.

As promised at the beginning of this chapter, we witnessed a near tragedy on I-95, close to Medway and on the way to New Brunswick. The incident began when I spotted a moose on the right-a-way approximately 150 yards in front. I decided to get a quick photo, after pulling over to a wide spot off the highway. Shortly after taking the photo and returning to the car, the moose decided to come back and cross the other side of the road. I immediately sensed the potential for an accident, so I waved the traffic to slow down and pull to a stop, and they

did – with one exception in the left lane. This driver made no attempt to slow down. Unfortunately, this was when the moose made its final attempt, to cross to the other side of the road. Leaving the aggressive driver, no time to stop the car before it was too late. Although the driver hit the brakes, the car skidded to the left, hitting the moose with the right side which broke out a window and caved in the entire right side of the automobile. Thankfully this accident was free of casualties. After a short time, the moose rallied to his feet and ran back into the woods, while the occupants of the damaged car where apparently shaken yet able to continue their journey in a car that was destined for a visit to the body shop. Given the positive outcome of this near tragedy, we were left wondering if this was an example of a divine intervention.

★ Kelly's Prespective & Lessons Learned ★

Looking forward to visiting Bar Harbor!

★ Famous People Born in Maine ★

Cyrus Curtis the publisher, born in Portland in 1850.

John Ford the film director, born in Cape Elizabeth in 1894.

Marsden Hartley the painter, born in Lewiston in 1877.

Henry Wadsworth Longfellow the poet, born in Portland in 1807.

Sarah Orne Jewett the author, born in South Berwick in 1849.

Stephen King the writer, born in Portland in 1947.

Linda Lavin the actress, born in Portland in 1937.

Hiram Stevens Maxim the inventor, born in Sangerville in 1840.

Marston Morse the mathematician, born in Waterville in 1892.

Frank Munsey the publisher, born in Mercer in 1854.

Walter Piston the composer, born in Rockland in 1894.

George Palmer Putnam the publisher, born in Brunswick in 1814.

Kenneth Roberts the historical author, born in Kennebunk in 1885.

Margaret Chase Smith the politician, born in Skowhegan in 1897.

Francis & Freelan Stanley the inventors, born in Kingfield in 1849.

John Hay Whitney the publisher, born in Ellsworth in 1904.

★ Where Will You Visit? ★

_____
_____
_____
_____

★ What Photos Will You Take? ★

_____
_____
_____
_____

State Capital: Annapolis

State Flower: Black-eyed Susan

Population: 5,773,552 (Ranks 19th, as of 2010 Census)

Land Area: 9707.2 square miles (Ranks 42nd)

Population Density: 594.8 persons per square mile (Ranks 5th)

★ Arlie's Insight & Highlights ★

Maryland is known as the "Old Line State", a nickname it received from heroics during the Revolutionary War. Another name given to Maryland includes the "Free State", first recognized on November 1, 1864, on that date, when slavery within the state's borders was abolished. It is also the state where Francis Scott Key was inspired to write the "Star Spangled Banner" as the British fired on Fort McHenry during the war of 1812. The rest of the nation can be thankful to Maryland's generosity for giving part of its land to the Federal Government in 1791, for the nation's capital, Washington D.C.

A brief review of early history of Maryland tells us the Spanish may be the first white explorers to visit the region, but never established a settlement as far North as Maryland. Around the time of Virginia's settlements by Captain John Smith 1608, he wrote of the area in Chesapeake Bay and mapped a portion of this area. By 1631, William Claiborne, had established a trading post on Kent Island, well up into the Chesapeake Bay area that would be just across the bay from the present city of Annapolis. Three years later, in 1634, the Englishman, Leonard Calvert founded the colony of Maryland on St. Clements Island, with about 150 settlers. Control of the Colony changed hands when in 1654, William Claiborne took command but only four year's later, Lord Baltimore regained control of the Colony. By the year 1691, England took direct control over the Maryland Colony. St. Clement Island was the site of the first Roman Catholic mass celebrated in the British-American colonies.

By 1715, the Baltimore's regained the colony of Maryland and much later in 1767 the disputed boundary of northern Maryland and southern Pennsylvania had been surveyed and completed by Mr. Mason and Mr. Dixon that was started in 1763.

It was in 1776 that Maryland declared its independence and the second Continental Congress met in Baltimore in 1776 – 1777. General George Washington resigned his commission as commander in chief of the military at Annapolis in 1783, after the Revolutionary War ended. Maryland became the seventh state in the union in April of 1788.

The geography of Maryland gets more complex after leaving the Atlantic coastal plains, which is an area on the east and west side of the Chesapeake Bay. When driving through this part of Virginia, Maryland and Delaware known as the "Delmarva Peninsula", it's all flat and beautiful farm country. As one goes west through central Maryland it blends into the Piedmont Region. From Hagerstown west, you encounter the Blue Ridge Mountains, father west you cross the Appalachian Ridges and Valleys into the Appalachian Plateau area. This is a beautiful drive if you like traveling through a variety of terrains.

Maryland is very important and supplies several agriculture products to the nation. Broiler chickens are one of the leading products followed by milk, eggs and hogs. The main land crop (cash crop) is corn grown over most of the state. Other important crops include: soybeans, wheat, peaches and tobacco.

During the War of 1812, several battles were fought on Maryland soil; its close proximity to Washington D.C. made it a convenient target for the British. The British raided many towns and farms along Chesapeake Bay during the summer of 1814. A large force commanded by British General Ross defeated American forces in the Battle of Bladensburg in August 1814. The British forces moved on to Washington D.C. at this time and burned the U.S. Capitol along with many other government buildings. In September of 1814, the British attacked Baltimore and fired on Fort McHenry, but the American forces defended the City of Baltimore and drove the British out of Maryland.

At the time of the Civil War (1861-1865), Maryland became a new battle ground. Maryland was a slave state, but when the war began in 1861, residences were divided in their loyalties between the north and the south. If Maryland joined the south (Confederacy), Washington D.C. would be surrounded by Confederate Territory. Maryland did decide to stay in the union, but many of the men joined the confederate cause. Many battles were fought in Maryland during this war. In 1862, General Lee's troops invaded Maryland and union forces fought them in the Battle of Antietam, near Sharpsburg, when more than 20,000 men were killed or wounded. In June 1863, General Lee's troops crossed Maryland into Pennsylvania, where he was defeated in the Battle of Gettysburg. In 1864, the Confederate General Jubal Anderson Early, crossed the Potomac River into Maryland very near Washington D.C., before union forces drove them back. This Civil War ended in May of 1865.

When you travel to Maryland, it would be prudent to spend a few days exploring the Chesapeake Bay area. There is a great deal of early history that occurred in this area, the surrounding states and nation's capital.

Specific places to see include: the first Capital of Maryland, near St. Mary's City, the Chesapeake Bay Maritime Museum, near St. Michaels, the U.S. Naval Academy of Annapolis, the Monocacy National Battlefield, near Sharpsburg, Harpers Ferry National Historic Park and George Washington's birthplace the National Monument on the Virginia side of the Potomac River. The drive from Fredrick west to Cumberland and to West Virginia is a beautiful drive for those that love to travel.

★ Famous People Born in Maryland ★

Spiro T. Agnew the vice president, born in Baltimore in 1918.

Benjamin Banneker the mathematician, astronomer, born in Oella/Ellicott City in 1731.

Christopher Gist the frontiersman, born in Baltimore in 1706.

Philip Glass the composer, born in Baltimore in 1937.

Matthew Henson the explorer, born in Charles City in 1866.

Johns Hopkins the financier, born in Anne Arundel City in 1795.

Francis Scott Key the lawyer, author, born in Carroll County. In 1779

Charles Willson Peale the painter, naturalist, born in Queen Annes City in 1741.

Babe Ruth the baseball player, born in Baltimore in 1895.

Upton Sinclair the author, born in Baltimore in 1878.

★ Where Will You Visit? ★

_____
_____
_____

★ What Photos Will You Take? ★

_____
_____
_____

State Capital: Boston

State Flower: Mayflower

Population: 6,547,629 (Ranks 14th, as of 2010 Census)

Land Area: 7,800.1 square miles (Ranks 45th)

Population Density: 839.4 persons per square mile (Ranks 3rd)

★ Arlie's Insight & Highlights ★

One of the most historic visits we have ever made to a state was Massachusetts. To explain this, one has to look into the early history of this state. Massachusetts could accurately be called "The State of Firsts", and is a place for one to see the beginning of America.

The *Mayflower* dropped anchor at Provincetown on November 11, 1620. Before they left the ship, these Pilgrims drew up a plan of self-government, known as the Mayflower Compact. The first library in the Colonies started in 1636, when John Harvard gave his book collection to Harvard College. Harvard is the first institute of higher learning in the U.S. The first telephone was invented by Alexander Graham Bell, in Boston in 1876. The first sewing machine was invented in Cambridge, by Elias Howe, in 1845, the first printing press was established in 1639 by Stephen Daye. The first successful iron works in North America started at Hammersmith (now Saugus) around 1646. The first real firefight was on British troops at Lexington and Concord in April of 1775. General George Washington first took charge of the army at Cambridge in July 1775. In early 1776, General Washington drove the British out of the Boston area; this was the first major victory for the colonists.

When one arrives in Massachusetts, it would be well to get a visitor's guide, a good map, and speak to some tour guides (more than one). Go to the Chamber of Commerce if it is handy. Most of the special historic sites are near the eastern shores in the state. Some tour services will take visitors from downtown Boston all the way to Provincetown, which is at the end of Cape Cod. There are many important points of history to see: Whaling Museum at New Bedford, Martha's Vineyard, Pilgrims Memorial Monument, Plimouth Plantation and Plymouth Rock, both at Plymouth. Closer to the Boston area, at Duxbury is the John Alden House, built in 1653. In the Boston general area, there are many historic sites: the Bunker Hill Memorial, the Adams National Historic Site, the Saugus Iron Works Historic Site, the *USS Constitution* (Old Ironsides) at the Boston Naval Base, Harvard University in Cambridge and the Minuteman Statue, at Lexington. The "Boston Tea Party" is one of the things that led to the outbreak of the Revolutionary War. Hammon Castle Museum, near Gloucester and the Fisherman's Memorial near the same location, is a worthy trip.

We spent one extra day in Boston, because we were told a certain guide knew the Ride of Paul Revere better than anyone in town; it was one of the most thorough narrations we have ever witnessed. Many historic sites can be accessed by driving to the location by automobile, so one can spend all the time necessary to fully enjoy history. Two locations that are such examples are Plymouth Rock and The Plimouth Plantation. In Plymouth, one can witness the *Mayflower II* that was built in Devon, England, ready to sail across the Atlantic Ocean on April 20, 1957. Built to the specifications of the original *Mayflower* at 106' long and 25' wide, it was to take the original voyage of the Mayflower. The Plimoth Plantation (e.g., Plimoth vs. Plymouth) was the big surprise to my wife. People were raising pigs and doing what they would have done in the 1620-1630. The plantation was a unique experience to see Pilgrim-type

dwellings and activities. This visit can be considered a hands-on experience, much different than a video or book narrative.

A boat trip around the Kennedy compound at Hyannis was an interesting experience. Here they provide ferry service to both Nantucket Island and Martha's Vineyard.

A ferry trip is available to Martha's Vineyard and services are available for touring the island. We had a great trip all the way west across the island, and stopped at Gay Head for lunch. We had a leisurely lunch break and I noticed two pair of mounted binoculars for observing the area for a fee. Before returning to the bus, the tour guide announced that there were two nude beaches just down the hill from where we were. Two lines formed quickly behind the two mounted binoculars and I was last in line!

An overview of the state, from a geographic standpoint, one would see the coastal lowlands, as the eastern part, the eastern New England upland, that east of the Connecticut River, for the center portion of the state and the western one-third of the state as the Western new England uplands. This western portion is more mountainous and is where one finds the ski areas, both north and south of the city of Pittsfield.

Eastern Massachusetts can be seen as the cradle of America. This is where mankind got some traction to survive in a strange land and harsh environment. According to the information plaque at the site, almost half the people died in the winter of 1620-21. They had very little food, crude shelters, and game was scarce.

The Pilgrims became friendly with the Indians and they helped them to plant corn and beans the following year, and this provided food the following winter. The Pilgrims celebrated their first Thanksgiving in 1621. A Thanksgiving Day for the purpose of prayer as well as celebration was decreed by Governor Bradford to take place on July 30, 1623.

My wife had the most fun at the Plimoth Plantation, where the dress code of the day was the subject. The actress portraying a colonist asked my wife if she was traveling alone, because she was wearing shorts. The lady told her it was dangerous to travel dressed as she was. My wife replied she was not alone, but with her husband. Other interesting observations at Plimoth Plantation were very interesting to the modern housewife. Women were observed peeling vegetables and fruit. They were cooking on wood stoves and canning the fruits. All people in the village were working at different activities. Men were building fences to keep pigs and goats from roaming. They were replicating the way things really were during Pilgrim Times.

★ Kelly's Perspective & Lessons Learned ★

The first time I had clam chowder was in Boston and it was during my first business trip. Wonderful memories that I have built on over the years with return trips to this historic city.

★ Famous People Born in Massachusetts ★

Susan B. Anthony the woman suffragist, born in Adams in 1820.

Clara Barton the American Red Cross founder, born in Oxford in 1821.

George H. W. Bush 41st U.S. president, born in Milton in 1924.

Bette Davis the actress, born in Lowell in 1908.

Cecil B. DeMille the film director, born in Ashfield in 1881.

Emily Dickinson the poet, born in Amherst in 1930.

Benjamin Franklin the statesman, scientist, born in Boston in 1706.

John Hancock the statesman, born in Braintree in 1737.

Nathaniel Hawthorne the author, born in Salem in 1804.

John F. Kennedy the 35th U.S. president, born in Brookline in 1917.

Christa McAuliffe the teacher, astronaut, born in Framingham in 1948.

Paul Revere the Revolutionary War figure, born in Boston in 1735.

Dr. Seuss - Theodore Geisel author, illustrator, born in Springfield in 1904.

★ Where Will You Visit? ★

_____

_____

_____

_____

★ What Photos Will You Take? ★

_____

_____

_____

_____

State Capital: Lansing

State Flower: Apple Blossom

Population: 9,883,640 (Ranks 8th, as of 2010 Census)

Land Area: 56,538.9 square miles (Ranks 22nd)

Population Density: 174.8 persons per square mile (Ranks 17th)

★ Arlie's Insight & Highlights ★

Originally Michigan was known as the Wolverine State, because of the early fur traders that brought the valuable wolverine pelts to the trading areas of this region. In more recent times, Michigan is better known for its manufacturing of the automo-

bile. Detroit, the largest city has been called the automobile capital of the world, or 'Motor City', although the automobile is also built in several other cities of southern Michigan that include; Dearborn, Flint, Pontiac, Lansing and Kalamazoo. The early period of the auto business began when Henry Ford built the first working automobile in 1896 at Detroit. Soon after, in 1899, Mr. Ransom Olds started the first automobile factory in the city of Detroit. Since those early days of the automobile development, it has had significant growth until July 18, 2013. On this day, Detroit's Chapter 9 bankruptcy petition, marking the largest municipal bankruptcy filing in history, sent the Motor City into unknown territory.

Taking a step back in time to the very early history of the region highlights the Indian occupation of the land that is now Michigan. It is estimated that approximately 15,000 Native Americans lived in the area and they consisted of several tribes that included Chippewa and Menominee on the Upper Peninsula, and Ottawa, Miami and Iroquois in the Lower Peninsula area.

The first foreigners to explore the region were the French. Father Jacques Marquette founded the first permanent settlement near Sault Ste. Marie, in 1668. In 1701, Antoine Cadillac settled at Fort Pontchartrain, that later became the City of Detroit. The main French interests were to convert the Native Indians to Christianity and maintain a profitable Fur Trade.

One important thing to keep in mind is, for many years, in the 15th and 16th century (1600's and 1700's) the French and British were in a constant struggle to control North America. French Settler's fought in many battles during the French and Indian Wars until finally the French were defeated in 1763. Although, the British got most of the previous French holding that included what is now Michigan, the Indian attacks never stopped. In 1774, the British made the area of Michigan part of The Province of Quebec. After the Revolutionary War, (1775-1783) the area of Michigan came under control of the United States. However, the British wanted the valuable fur trade as long as possible, so they did not give up Detroit or Fort Mackinac to the United States until 1796, long after the Revolutionary War ended.

In 1787, the Michigan area became part of the Northwest Territory and in 1800, Congress created the Indiana Territory, which included part of Michigan and in 1803 the Indiana Territory acquired the entire Michigan Region. By 1805, Congress created the Territory of Michigan, upper and lower Peninsulas. In 1837, Michigan became the 26th state in January of that year and Michigan was complete, including all of the upper peninsula. Another red letter day occurred in 1854, when the

Republican Party was formally named at Jackson, Michigan. The party started a series of anti-slavery meetings throughout the north that same year.

In addition to being the key location for the auto industry, the famous inventor, Thomas Edison built his first electric battery at what is now Port Huron, in 1861. Michigan appeared to be the center of some important inventions in early America. However, it appears the Henry Ford effort to build a better automobile affected more Americans than any other endeavor in history. The visitor to Dearborn can experience much of this at Greenfield Village in suburban Detroit, where a collection of historic buildings have been restored by the Ford Family. When we visited the Henry Ford Museum and the Greenfield Village, we were surprised to see buildings restore relating to such famous persons as Stephen Foster, Abraham Lincoln, William McGuffey and Thomas Edison. This place is an important landmark that visitors will enjoy. Northern Michigan also has special sights such as the International Bridge at Sault Ste. Marie along with four U.S. Soo Locks that allow ships to travel between Lake Huron and Lake Superior.

On the shore of Lake Michigan, the visitor can find many state parks to enjoy beginning at the Indiana border all the way north to the "Sleeping Bear Dunes National Lakeshores". Although we never traveled Michigan in the winter months, we have heard of good ski areas in the northern part of the state, some that come to mind are; Sugar Loaf Ski Resort, Boyne Mountain Ski area and Boyne Highlands Ski Area. If the Detroit area is on your agenda, there are many points of interest, in and around the area to spend time visiting.

We spent a few days in and around the Detroit and Windsor Canada area, because there is so much to see. The Lake tour on the "Star of Detroit" for lunch and cruise on Lake St. Clair

will be etched in our memories forever, because of the awesome scenery and the photos we have of this tour. On this tour one can view the City, Belle Isle Park and Grosse Pointe Woods area of northeast Detroit, all magnificent scenery. The Edsel and Eleanor Ford House (estate) is a tour that visitors will certainly enjoy. Edsel Ford, the president of the Ford Motor Company for many years and his wife Eleanor completed this 87 acre estate in 1927. Edsel was the creator of the Ford Foundation in 1936. He died here in 1943, but his wife who lived here until her death in October, 1976, endowed the property and directed it be maintained for public use, otherwise we may never have been able to see and enjoy this great estate. Several photo opportunities presented themselves during this visit, along with one of my wife standing in the doorway of the children's play house, which turned out to be another wonderful experience.

Michigan is unique in many ways, but its location is different geographically, the state borders on four of the five Great Lakes,

Superior, Michigan, Huron and Lake Erie. The state comes in two parts, the Upper and Lower Peninsula and the entire area was covered by Glaciers at one time. The Land Region consists of the Great Lakes Plains and the Superior Upland — all important reasons to visit the beautiful state of Michigan.

★ Kelly's Perspective & Lessons Learned ★

Traveling to Michigan took on new meaning when my dear friend Melissa moved to the state with her family. This relocation gave me another important reason to visit the charming city of Plymouth.

★ Famous People Born in Michigan ★

Roger Chaffee the astronaut, born in Grand Rapids in 1935.

Francis Ford Coppola the film director, born in Detroit in 1939.

Thomas E. Dewey the politician, born in Owosso in 1902.

Earvin Magic Johnson the basketball player, born in Lansing in 1959.

Charles A. Lindbergh the aviator, born in Detroit in 1902.

Madonna the singer, born in Bay City in 1958.

Dick Martin the comedian, born in Detroit in 1922.

Gilda Radner the comedian, born in Detroit in 1946.

Diana Ross the singer, born in Detroit in 1944.

Steven Seagal the actor, born in Lansing in 1952.

Tom Selleck the actor, born in Detroit in 1949.

Lily Tomlin the actress, born in Detroit in 1939.

Stevie Wonder the singer, born in Saginaw in 1950.

★ Where Will You Visit? ★

★ What Photos Will You Take? ★

State Capital: St. Paul

State Flower: Pink and White Lady's Slipper

Population: 5,303,925 (Ranks 21st, as of 2010 Census)

Land Area: 79,626.7 square miles (Ranks 31st)

Population Density: 66.6 persons per square mile (Ranks 32nd)

★ Arlie's Insight & Highlights ★

Minnesota is known as the Gopher State, because of the many gophers that live in the prairies of the southern part of the state. Another nickname that may be more appropriate is the bread and butter state. Background: Minnesota grows a variety of crops and produces a great deal of cattle as well as hogs. The most common crops include: corn, soybeans, hay, flaxseed, sugar beets and potatoes. Once the flour mills process and other refinements are made, the final consumer products can resemble a mini bread basket.

The state is also well known as a producer of iron ore from the Mesabi and Vermillion Ranges located in the northeastern part of Minnesota. Interestingly, more than half of the U.S. iron ore comes from Minnesota. Other useful commodities from the state include timber products from the thick forest of pines that attracted the lumberjacks in the early development of Minnesota. The symbols are still present at Brainerd's Paul Bunyan amusement center, Lumbertown USA as well as at Paul Bunyan and Blue-Ox statue.

Taking a look back at the early days of Minnesota's history, gives us a picture of turmoil for much of the Midwest. The struggle was among the French, the British and the Native Americans. The foreigners exploring part of Minnesota in the late 1600's, found the Sioux raising some crops and hunting the wild game of the area. By 1750, the Chippewa were moving west into what is now Minnesota.

When the Chippewa moved west, it forced the Sioux to move to the southwest and the Sioux became nomadic because they could not coexist and the two tribes remained enemies for many years. The French fur traders appeared to be the first foreigners to explore the area of Minnesota around 1600. More Frenchmen came into the area about 1679, one known as Seiur Duluth, hoped to blaze a trail all the way to the Pacific Ocean. He claimed this entire region for King Louis XIV of France. In 1680, a Belgian, Louis Hennepin set out to explore the upper Mississippi River, but was captured by the Indians only to be released at a later date. Hennepin became the first foreigner to visit what is now Minneapolis and named the Falls of St. Anthony.

At the end of the French and Indian War in 1763, France lost the war and as a result, France gave Britain most of its land east of the Mississippi River, including eastern Minnesota. At the end of the Revolutionary War (1776-1783), Great Britain gave its land south of the Great Lakes and east of the Mississippi River to the U.S. and this large area became part of the Northwest Territory, which Congress created in 1787. In 1803, the United States got control of western Minnesota through the Louisiana Purchase from France. Exploration by Henry Schoolcraft, in 1832 led to the discovery of Lake Itasca, the source of the Mississippi River.

By 1837, the Sioux and Chippewa gave up more of their land through sales in the St. Croix Valley and by 1849 congress created the Minnesota Territory. In 1851, the Indians gave up their rights to large tracts of land west of the Mississippi River and in May of 1858 Minnesota became the 32nd state in the Union.

The geography of Minnesota is not complex but different than most states, as the Superior Upland is made of very hard rock like much of eastern Canada, known as the Canadian Shield. The Young Drift Plains covers much of the good soil in Minnesota and two other areas small in size are the Driftless area and Till Plains of southwestern Minnesota.

What first sparked our interest in Minnesota, was the research for great musky fishing. This state is truly the land of 10,000 lakes. The northern part of Minnesota is just a paradise for the outdoor person. The area around Leech Lake, is as far north as we ventured, but it was fascinating for us to learn how the Minnesota Indians harvest wild rice, as they do it much the same way their ancestors did.

From Minneapolis we toured the Mississippi River North to what we were told was the head of navigation on the river. We took a number of photos to remember the area and experience of going through the large locks and dams on the river.

For the visitor to Minnesota, there are many sites outside the St. Paul area, but one should considering spending a few days in the central location to get the full enjoyment of the parks and city atmosphere. In the northern part of the state, the visitor will find Lake of the Woods, for fishing in the wild, the Voyageurs National Park, near International Falls, Paul Bunyan and Blue Ox Statue, near Bemidji, Lumbertown USA and Paul Bunyan Amusement Center both near Brainerd. In southern Minnesota, it is mainly an agricultural area, although some sites are worth visiting. Near Granite Falls is Wood Lake St. Monument as well as Schwandt St. Monument and near Pipestone, one will find Pipestone National Monument on the border of South Dakota.

If you have ever enjoyed the wilderness, traveling through northern Minnesota will bring back those memories. On this trip I personally had a wonderful case of nostalgia!

★ Famous People Born in Minneapolis ★

LaVerne, Maxene, and Patti Andrews the singers, born in Minneapolis in 1918.

Bob Dylan the singer, composer, born in Duluth in 1941.

Francis Scott Fitzgerald the author, born in Saint Paul in 1896.

Judy Garland the singer, actress, born in Grand Rapids in 1922.

Garrison Keillor the humorist, born in Anoka in 1942.

Jessica Lange the actress, born in Cloquet in 1949.

John Madden the sportscaster, born in Austin in 1936.

Roger Maris the baseball player, born in Hibbing in 1934.

Charles Horace the Mayo surgeon, born in Rochester in 1865.

William J. Mayo the surgeon, born in Le Sueur in 1861.

Prince Rogers Nelson singer, born in Minneapolis in 1958.

Charles Schulz the cartoonist, born in Minneapolis in 1922.

★ Where Will You Visit? ★

_____
_____
_____
_____

★ What Photos Will You Take? ★

_____
_____
_____
_____

State Capital: Jackson

State Flower: Magnolia

Population: 2,967,297 (Ranks 31st, as of 2010 Census)

Land Area: 46,923.3 square miles (Ranks 32nd)

Population Density: 63.2 persons per square mile (Ranks 20th)

★ **Arlie's Insight & Highlights** ★

Mississippi is one of the southern states with many well preserved residences known as Antebellum homes. If 'Antebellum' is a new term to you, know that it is Latin in origin and refers to the architecture style (prewar) which is the neoclassical design characteristic of the 19th-century Southern United States. Because we enjoy the style, it was easy to visit many of the Antebellum homes found in Natchez, Vicksburg, Gulfport, Biloxi and Jackson during our trip. Although we feel sure there are many at other locations across the state, we were able to visit a cross section of homes and recommend these destinations to all that enjoy this style. Further, the historic mansions hold memories of the plantation life before and during the Civil War. Other memories include the beautiful magnolia trees and the graceful magnolia leaves we bought and later painted gold for our Christmas decorations – which we still have to this day.

From an agricultural lens, Mississippi produces many crops that are beneficial to locals and the nation. They grow soybeans, sugar cane, sweet potatoes, as well as cotton. Residents also raise a significant amount of beef and dairy cattle. If you are on vacation, it will be clear that the tourism industry thrives along the coastal areas. This is what happens when you combine several nice beach areas and a great climate, with lots of memorable southern cooking. The visitor to Mississippi should be prepared to drive many miles in order to enjoy all the history the state has to offer, but first it will be necessary to take a brief look back to the areas early days.

Like the other states in America, the Mississippi region was occupied with the Native American Indians. It is estimated that 25,000 to 30,000 Indians lived in what is now Mississippi, before the white explorers came to the land. Some of the dominant tribes were; Natchez, Choctaw Chickasaw and others.

In the very early years, it was Hernando De Soto that came to the Mississippi region in about 1540. Despite this, the Spanish found no treasures and made no settlements. Much later, in 1682, the French explorer Robert Cavelier, came down from the Canadian area on the Mississippi River and claimed the entire valley for France and named it Louisiana, the region included what is now the state of Mississippi. In 1699, the first French settlement of the area was at "Old Biloxi". Later in 1716, the second settlement was made by Jean Baptiste at Rosalie, (what is now Natchez). Three years later, the first slaves were brought in from West Africa, to work the fields of the French Colonies. Early capitals for Louisiana Territory were old Biloxi, New Biloxi and Fort Louis De La Mobile (now Mobile, Alabama) during the early 1700's. However, in 1722, the French made New Orleans, Louisiana the capital of this entire region. The Louisiana Territory made up a large region from the eastern Allegheny Mountains to the Rocky Mountains in the west. In 1736, British troops helped some Indians (Chickasaw) defeat the French Colonists in the north that kept the French from gaining control of the Mississippi Valley. During the time of the French and Indian War (1754-1763) the British and Chickasaw kept the French of the lower Mississippi from joining the French of the Ohio valley area. After the treaty that ended the war, the British got all the land east of the Mississippi River and all this region came under British control. This was later split into Western Florida and part of the Georgia Colony.

During the Revolutionary War, most of the people of west Florida were loyal to the British, but some elements of the population (Indians and Trappers) supported the colonies. In 1781, Britain granted West Florida to Spain. However, after the British lost in the Revolutionary War, the Mississippi region north of the 32nd parallel became part of the United States. In 1798, Congress organized the Mississippi territory and Natchez became the capital. In 1803, the Louisiana Purchase made the Mississippi River a part of the United States.

During the war of 1812, the Choctaw Indians helped General

Andrew Jackson in defeating the British Army in the Battle of New Orleans. In 1817, congress split the Mississippi Territory into the State of Mississippi and Alabama Territory and on December 10, 1817, Mississippi became the 20th State of the Union.

Before the Civil War began, there was much turmoil and tension in the United States over the slavery issue. In January of 1861, a meeting was held in Jackson for Mississippi to secede from the union and Mississippi became the second state to secede, after South Carolina. A short time later, Jefferson Davis of Mississippi became president of the Confederacy. During the Civil War, Mississippi was an area of many battles and the state suffered many losses of property and people. The battle at Vicksburg was one of the most important of the war. Note-

worthy, Vicksburg was under siege for almost two months before it fell.

The fall of Vicksburg to General Grant's forces on July 4, 1863, gave the union control of the Mississippi River. In fact, the union victories at Vicksburg and Gettysburg were the turning point of the Civil War. In 1867, after the war, the United States put Mississippi under military control during the reconstruction period. In 1870, Mississippi was re-admitted to the union, but it took many years for the state to recover from the losses of this war.

The geography of Mississippi is reasonably simple, it's two basic features of land formations are; the Mississippi Alluvial Plain and the Gulf Costal Plains, with a small portion of "Black Belt" that extends out of Alabama in the northeastern portion of the state.

The visitor to Mississippi has a variety of choices to explore today: from great beaches, exciting river cruises or just the inland travel to the historic sites. There are many Antebellum homes in the Natchez area open for tours, to name a few; The Rosalie, Stanton Hall, Linden, Melrose, Auburn, Edgewood and Dunleith.

Our Experiences in Mississippi have been many, but the most rewarding were the visits to all the Antebellum homes in different locations around the state. We hope each visitor to Mississippi receives as much joy and many pleasant surprises as they explore this great state.

★ Famous People Born in Mississippi ★

Jimmy Buffett the singer, songwriter, born in Pascagoula in 1946.

Brett Farve the football player, born in Kiln in 1969.

William Faulkner the author, born in New Albany in 1897.

Jim Henson the puppeteer, born in Greenville in 1936.

Faith Hill the singer, born in Jackson in 1967.

James Earl Jones the entertainer, born in Arkabutla in 1931.

B. B. King the guitarist, born in Itta Bena in 1925.

Walter Payton the football player, born in Columbia in 1953.

Elvis Presley the singer, actor, born in Tupelo in 1935.

Jerry Rice the football player, born in Starkville in 1962.

Conway Twitty the country musician, born in Friars Point in 1933.

Sela Ward the actress, Meridian in 1956.

Tennessee Williams the playwright, born in Columbus in 1911.

Oprah Winfrey the talk-show host, born in Kosciusko in 1954.

★ **Where Will You Visit?** ★

_____
_____
_____
_____

★ **What Photos Will You Take?** ★

_____
_____
_____
_____

State Capital: Jefferson City

State Flower: Hawthorne

Population: 5,988,927 (Ranks 18th, as of 2010 Census)

Land Area: 68,741.5 square miles (Ranks 18th)

Population Density: 87.1 persons per square mile (Ranks 28th)

★ Arlie's Insight & Highlights ★

The song, "Missouri, I hear you callin' me, my heart will yearn, 'til I return, Missouri's callin' me" is a favorite tune of mine. Also the words are reflective of what has happened to me in excess of forty-five times, as of this writing. Yes, we really did visit the state in the spring and fall months for fourteen consecutive years. The locations we visited with motor home and travel trailer are: Branson, on the River (Lake Taneycomo), Bennett Springs State Park, Meramec Springs, (near Stanton), Montauk State Park, (near Licking) and roaring River State Park, (near Cassville).

One can tell from these areas that trout fishing is one of the main activities at these locations (with the exception of Branson). Branson is a complete vacation in one spot and is one of the most visited spots in the entire nation. It has day and night music, comedy, night cruises and great restaurants. Travel in and around the area is easy. Missouri has some dramatic history in its past. We can start with one of my favorite stories; the story of Lewis and Clark's Journey to the northwest in 1804. Another "Red Letter" Day was the Missouri compromise of 1821 which brought Missouri into the Union. The Dred Scott decision by the Supreme Court in 1857 prevented this Missouri slave from gaining his freedom and all slaves from becoming US citizens. This was one of the events that led to the civil war. Although it lasted only 18 months in 1860, the Pony Express provided fast mail delivery between St. Joseph, Missouri, and Sacramento, California.

In the mid-1800s two major trail heads, The Santa Fe Trail and the Oregon Trail, began in Independence, Missouri, causing it to be known as the "Gateway to the West". After the Civil War, the main "bad guy" was Jesse James, who terrorized the state for many years. The early history of Missouri is found in more details in the many museums across the state.

Missouri has large amounts of river frontage. The Mississippi River forms the eastern border of the state where tourists can still ride the old stern-wheel boats up and down this mighty river. The Missouri River runs through the northern part of the state and it has river activity all the way to Kansas City on the western border.

Missouri has many smaller rivers that are beautiful recreation areas for fishing and camping. Some we have visited and enjoyed are; the White, Eleven Point, the Current, the Meramec, Roaring, and the James River.

Missouri has many caves scattered across the Ozark Plateau. Some of the best-known are Crystal Caverns, Marvel Cave, Fantastic Cavern, Onyx Caverns, and Meramac, Missouri has many large lakes and recreation areas. Most of the largest lakes are south and west of Jefferson City, including Lake of the Ozarks, Harry S. Truman Reservoir, Stockton Lake, Pomme de Terre, and Table Rock Lake, near Branson. Missouri has some of the best outdoor recreation areas in the region.

Southern Missouri has several beautiful, large, springs flowing right up out of the ground. We have enjoyed Big Springs, Bennett Springs, Meramec Springs., Blue Springs, and Montauk Springs. The cold water below these springs provides some good trout fishing, where trout are stocked.

After leaving the countryside of the Ozarks, the two major cities are St. Louis and Kansas City. In St. Louis, is the Gateway Arch on the river bank is an engineering marvel and one can see photos and illustrations showing how it went together. A small rail inside will take one to the top, where there are tiny windows looking over the city. The climatron at the Missouri Botanical Gardens is beautiful and a great place for lots of photos. St. Louis also has numerous museums of art and culture.

Hannibal, Missouri is the home and museum of Mark Twain. One can also visit the Mark Twain Cave, the old playground of the writer, where he may have found some of the inspiration to write *The Adventures of Tom Sawyer*.

As we move up the Missouri River, to Kansas City, the visitor will experience some new history. The most interesting for us was the Independence area, where one finds the Harry S. Truman Library. This library holds millions of documents about U.S. relations with foreign countries. The visitor can also view the graves of President Truman and his wife, Bess.

★ Kelly's Perspective & Lessons Learned ★

Although I have visited the greater Branson area over time, we recently returned for a family gathering and we were shocked at the growth. The good news is the expansion has brought additional activities and new entertainment to this special part of Missouri.

★ Famous People Born in Missouri ★

Yogi Berra the baseball player, born in Saint Louis in 1925.

George Washington Carver the educator and agricultural chemist, born in Diamond Grove in 1864.

Samuel Langhorne Clemens (Mark Twain) the author, born in Florida in 1835.

Walter Cronkite the TV newscaster, born in Saint Joseph in 1916.

Redd Foxx the actor and comedian, born in Saint Louis in 1922.

Betty Grable the actress, born in Saint Louis in 1916.

Edwin Hubble the astronomer, born in Marshfield in 1889.

James Langston Hughes the poet, born in Joplin in 1902.

Jesse James the outlaw, born in Centerville in 1847.

Shannon Miller the Olympic gymnast, born in Rolla in 1977.

James C. Penney the merchant, born in Hamilton in 1875.

Ginger Rogers the dancer and actress, born in Independence in 1911.

Casey Stengel the baseball player, born in Kansas City in 1890.

Harry S. Truman the 33rd U.S. president, born in Lamar in 1884.

Dick Van Dyke the actor, born in West Plains in 1925.

★ Where Will You Visit? ★

_____
_____
_____
_____

★ What Photos Will You Take? ★

_____
_____
_____
_____

State Capital: Helena

State Flower: Bitterroot

Population: 989,415 (Ranks 44th, as of 2010 Census)

Land Area: 145,545.8 square miles (Ranks 4th)

Population Density: 6.8 persons per square mile (Ranks 48th)

★ Arlie's Insight & Highlights ★

Montana, also known as the "Treasure State," holds a special place in my memories. It is the state where I worked at my first real job away from home. I was fortunate to have help from my biology teacher that had previous experience with the U.S. Forest Service in the state of Montana. After acquiring an application for the U.S. Forest Service and filling out all the necessary paperwork I got five of my teachers to write a short narrative as character witness for me. I will forever be grateful to those teachers. It is important to understand the history of Montana's beginnings on the road to being the 41st state in the union. The state's name came from the Spanish word "mountainous," however; the Spanish did not appear to have had much influence this far north as they did farther south and west in the United States. The French trappers may have seen parts of Montana as early as the mid-1700s but the recorded information came with the Lewis and Clark expedition across the region during 1805 and their return trip in 1806. After Lewis and Clark, the fur traders became very active in the area and by 1847 the American Fur Company built a permanent settlement at Fort Benton on the Missouri River. The United States acquired most of what is now Montana through the Louisiana Purchase, in 1803, from France. The northwestern part was acquired by treaty from England in 1846.

At many times in the past, Montana has been part of various territories: Idaho, Washington, Oregon, Dakota, Louisiana, and Missouri. In the territorial days many battles were fought with the Native Americans. One must remember that different tribes of Native Americans lived all over this region and when the white men came and began to move the Natives around they were angry and began to retaliate. This resulted in war.

In fact, two of the most famous battles that ever happened between the Native Americans and the U.S. Military occurred in Montana. In June 1876 the Cheyenne and Sioux Indians surprised General Custer at the Little Bighorn River and wiped out his entire regiment; this battle is known as "Custer's Last Stand." To see this place is very emotional; we have done this location three times.

Another serious encounter with the Native Americans was

when the government tried to move the Nez Perce Indians from their Oregon lands. They were on their way to Canada, but General Miles captured them after a two-day battle at Big Hole in southwestern Montana. After the Nez Perce Battle things began to settle down with the Native American Indians and the surrender of Chief Joseph in 1877. After the fighting ended, Montana's population grew rapidly. The railroads came and Montana became the 41st state in November of 1889.

Montana's geography comes in two basic land regions, the eastern two-thirds consist of the Great Plains, basically flat and rolling terrain and the western one-third is beautiful mountains of all sizes separated by great rivers and valleys; this is some of the most beautiful terrain one can find in any of the fifty states in America. Many of the farms in eastern Montana average 2,500 acres or more and the ranches are very large in the state, averaging several thousand acres. Some of the main

crops are wheat, barley, sugar beets, potatoes and hay crops. The main livestock are cattle, sheep, and hogs.

For the visitor to Montana, there are many options, especially if one is a hunter, fisherman, or camper. For the hunter, there are antelope on the plains and deer, bear, elk, mountain goat and mountain sheep in the high mountains. The fisherman has some of the best trout fishing in the U.S. in mountain streams and lakes of the state. Sight-seeing is exciting everywhere if you enjoy nature and outdoor life. Some special places to visit are the Yellowstone National Park area, the Custer Battlefield National Monument, the Big-hole National Battlefield, and Glacier National Park, with majestic mountain scenery, is like a fantasy land to the traveler. Other sights of interest would be the museum of the Plains Indian at Browning, the Lewis and Clark Memorial, and Virginia City.

My first experience and arrival in the state of Montana was when I got the job with the forest service. My teacher had previous employment with the Forest Service and he knew where to go and what we had to do to prepare for the job. The trip was a pleasant one, enjoying all the scenery, anticipating the new job, and my first chance to travel this far from home. Our first stop in the state of Montana was at the Crow Agency and a visit to the Little Bighorn Battlefield National Memorial. The next stop was at my teacher's family home in Big Timber, where they made me feel welcome for three wonderful days, before we journeyed on to the Libby, Montana ranger station.

Upon my arrival at the ranger station, I was processed and assigned to various areas of the Kootenai National Forest in northwest Montana. I had training on specific vegetation to look for, certain firefighting techniques and how to chip, saw, and prepare camp wood as well as how to saw down and notch a tree to fall a certain place. I was assigned to the Big Cherry Creek camp south of Libby, Montana. Our camp would consist of twelve to fifteen people, including a camp cook, the camp boss, and assistant.

The camp at Cherry Creek turned out to be a blessing and a great place to work from. The primary duty of each worker was to find and destroy certain species of goose berry or current plants that causes blister rust on the white pine trees. Life and the job went well at Big Cherry Creek Camp, except for some bear encounters near our garbage pit. It was a hot, dry, summer until one late evening in mid-July a lightning storm, though not much rain, came over the mountains to our west and started thirty eight fires. This was a great surprise to us Neophyte Employees of the forest service. Many of the fires were quickly extinguished by firefighters from several sources, but the strikes high in the mountains simmered before being detected, because duff and pine needles are like a thick carpet on the ground where a fire can creep for hours before a breakout.

We got the assignment on a high mountain strike, on Indian Head Peak, several miles away.

With fire packs ready and food and water supplies loaded on the forest service truck, we drove to the road's end and put on our fire packs and hit the trail into the wilderness. We hiked all night up Indian Head Peak looking for the fire we were to extinguish. Finally in late morning, my boss communicated with a distant lookout by walkie-talkie and we received help locating this fire. Luckily, the fire had burned less than one acre under tall timber and had never broken out. After the end of the day digging out old stumps and making a fire perimeter the fire was out. Due to the Forest Service rule at the time, we had to stay 24 hours after the last smoke occurred. Our food and rations ran out. We were hungry and I was elected to take water bags and go down the mountain to the nearest stream and bring back drinking water. The snow and ice on top of the mountain was frozen and too dirty for drinking.

Our summer at Cherry Creek was always exciting. We were assigned to do more firefighting. Most were small fires and we were designated as "smoke chasers" to catch them before they got out of control. We did go on one large fire where we got help from "smoke jumpers" out of Missoula, Montana. This large fire was near Quartz Mountain and the Forest Service used everything to control it. We had smoke jumpers, smoke chases and bulldozers where possible. I learned how to use controlled backfires. Our area to control was high and we ran out of food and water again; it was two days before they gave us a water and food drop. As you may imagine, it was a great surprise, when we heard and spotted the Trimotor Ford aircraft that brought us food and water. Although this was the first and last time I saw this aircraft - it was a welcome sight.

Our great summer seasonal duties ended at the Cherry Creek Camp and I was accepted as a regular duty employee for further employment. A change of location was next. I reported to the Troy Ranger District and went on "Spruce Survey" duty up the Yaak River and across to American Creek. We were packed in seven miles from the nearest road.

The last location, American Creek, is two miles from the British Columbian border north and two miles from the Idaho border west.

The fall season had arrived and the military duty was approaching for me so I had to make a choice; I elected to join the U.S. Army for three years after returning home. I could not help but remember the Forest Service job that was such an intense part of my life that year. I have returned to Montana several times, to hunt and on business, but nothing could ever compare to that earlier job in the Kootenai National Forest. The last trip to Montana was to look at an oil and gas lease near Havre, Montana, but I could not resist a trip to Libby and Big Cherry Creek, where I had to share stories with my wife about my earlier experiences in this mystical part of the state.

★ Kelly's Perspective & Lessons Learned ★

During the last visit to Yellowstone, we learned that Montana has the largest grizzly bear population in the lower 48 states and spotted one!

★ Famous People Born in Montana ★

Dorothy Baker the author, born in Missoula in 1907.

Dirk Benedict the actor, born in Helena in 1945.

Gary Cooper the actor, born in Helena in 1901.

Chet Huntley the journalist, TV newscaster, born in Cardwell in 1911.

Phil D. Jackson the basketball player and coach, born in Deer Lodge in 1945.

Will James the writer and artist, born in Great Falls in 1892.

Evel Knievel the daredevil motorcyclist, born in Butte in 1938.

Jerry Kramer the football player and author, born in Jordan in 1936.

Myrna Loy the actress, born in Helena in 1905.

David Lynch the filmmaker, born in Missoula in 1946.

George Montgomery the actor, born in Brady in 1916.

Jeannette Rankin the first woman elected to Congress, born in Missoula in 1880.

Martha Raye the actress, born in Butte in 1916.

★ Where Will You Visit? ★

★ What Photos Will You Take? ★

State Capital: Lincoln

State Flower: Goldenrod

Population: 1,826,341 (Ranks 38th, as of 2010 Census)

Land Area: 76,824.2 square miles (Ranks 15th)

Population Density: 23.8 persons per square mile (Ranks 43rd)

★ Arlie's Insight & Highlights ★

Nebraska, also known as the Cornhusker State, is unique in some respects that I look forward to explaining in more detail in this chapter. In the meantime and before I ever visited the state of Nebraska, I will always remember the great football rivalry between Oklahoma and Nebraska! It was a perennial challenge for both of these talented college football teams.

This was more personal for me than most. Since the Western Electric (now AT&T) plant closed in Lincoln, and many of the employees transferred to AT&T in Oklahoma City. As a result, I had several neighbors and co-workers from Nebraska! After getting to know many of them, I confess we had great fun and I have never met a Nebraskan I didn't like. I have always admired the tough, strong willed people of the Midwest.

From a historical lens, the state name is said to come from the Oto Indian word Nebrathka, which means 'Flatwater' and that describes the Platte River inside of Nebraska. Before state settlement, Nebraska, like other parts of the Midwest, was Indian country occupied by many different tribes of Native Americans. Some of the tribes of the region were the Oto, Ponca, Omaha and the Missouri who lived and hunted along the rivers of this region. These early Indians even farmed corn, beans and other crops. The Pawnee were friendly with the white settlers and helped the army scout against the Sioux, their (Pawnee's) enemy for many years. Some of the others tribes of the western part of this region were the: Arapaho, Comanche, Sioux and Cheyenne were hunting nomads that built no villages and did not cultivate the land.

The plains Indians from Nebraska's western region, were more hostile to the settlers, due to encroachment on their hunting areas. This problem existed in general until after the 1870's. Many of Nebraska's Native Indians now live on reservations as they do in other states, like Oklahoma and Arizona.

In 1803, the United States purchased the Louisiana Territory from France and this was included in what is now Nebraska. More extensive exploration occurred after the Louisiana Purchase. Louis and Clark did the most extensive exploration beginning in 1804 and continued through 1806. Zebulon Pike visited southern Nebraska during 1806. In 1813, Robert Stewart led his party up the Platte Rivers across Nebraska and by 1819 the U.S. Military established Fort Atkinson on the Missouri River, north of present-day Omaha, Nebraska. The route explored by Robert Stuart in his early travels, became known as the Oregon Trail later and was traveled by those for 50 years heading west to Oregon. Another famous trail inside of Nebraska's borders includes the Mormon Trail that runs north of the Platte River. The 'Great Migration' started up the Oregon Trail during the 1840's and this went through Nebraska from east to west. Up until 1854, part of the state was described as the Great American Desert by some, but in 1854, Congress passed the Kansas-Nebraska Act, creating the Nebraska Territory and people began to move in.

In 1862, the Congress passed the Homestead Act, which gave free land (160 acres) to frontier settler, this boosted populations greatly. By March 1, 1867 Nebraska became the 37th state in the union.

In 1934, the people of Nebraska voted to have a unicameral legislature (a single legislature) which is the only one I know of in our fifty states.

The geography of Nebraska is a very simple overall land form. The western 80% consist of the 'Great Plains' and the eastern 20% represents the dissected till plains. The western portion is a great ranching region, while the eastern part is great farm country, but like all things, there are always exceptions and the river bottoms (of the west) grow a variety of crops. They are certainly helped by the irrigation from the rivers and dams made for this purpose, as extra water can change land use in many ways.

For the visitor to Nebraska, one needs to be prepared to drive many miles to enjoy this state, because it is quite large. We have traveled I-80 from Omaha west to the Wyoming border and highway 183 from Kansas to South Dakota, but many sights will be off the main roads, so make a plan and use a good map to enjoy this state. Some places of interest in southeast Nebraska would be; Homestead National Monument of America, near Beatrice and the Willa Cather State Historic site near, Red Cloud.

In central Nebraska, near Gothenburg, the area is home to the old 'Pony Express Station' where riders picked up fresh horses to continue their journey. This landmark is on the old Oregon Trail that followed the Platte River through Nebraska. Another site near North Platte, Nebraska is Fort Cody and Buffalo Bill Ranch State Historic Park. In western Nebraska there are several sites to see they are; Courthouse and Jail Rocks, near Bridgeport, Chimney Rock, nearby and Scotts Bluff National Monument, near Gering. In the northwest corner of the state, near Harrison is the "Agate Fossil Beds National Monument" and near Chadron, is the museum of the fur trade.

One very large land feature is the Nebraska Sand Hills, a memorable sight worth visiting. Between North Platte and Valentine is a good road to travel to see part of this sight. Nebraska has many state parks and this is great for visitors pulling trailers and other RV's.

A personal thought about the state of Nebraska, is that this state may be over looked by many vacationers, because they don't know what the state has to offer in the Great Plaines of America. Go ahead, be bold and enjoy exploring this great state as much as we do.

★ Famous People Born in Nebraska ★

Grover Cleveland Alexander the baseball pitcher, born in Saint Paul in 1887.

Fred Astaire the dancer and actor, born in Omaha in 1899.

Max Baer the boxer, born in Omaha in 1909.

Marlon Brando the actor, born in Omaha in 1924.

Warren Buffett the investor, born in Omaha in 1930.

Henry Fonda the actor, born in Grand Island in 1905.

Gerald Rudolph Ford 37th U.S. president, born in Omaha in 1913.

Hoot Gibson the actor, born in Tememah in 1892.

Frank W. Leahy the football coach, born in O'Neill in 1908.

Nick Nolte the actor, born in Omaha 1941.

Red Cloud the Indian rights advocate and leader, born near North Platte in 1822.

Standing Bear the Indian rights advocate and leader, born along the Niobrara River in 1893.

Darryl F. Zanuck the film producer, born in Wahoo in 1902.

★ Where Will You Visit? ★

_____

_____

_____

_____

★ What Photos Will You Take? ★

_____

_____

_____

_____

State Capital: Carson City

State Flower: Sagebrush

Population: 2,700,551 (Ranks 35th, as of 2010 Census)

Land Area: 109,781.2 square miles (Ranks 7th)

Population Density: 24.6 persons per square mile (Ranks 42nd)

★ Arlie's Insight & Highlights ★

Nevada, the silver state, holds a strange fascination for me. The paradox is that it has some of the brightest night-life in Las

Vegas and Reno, yet some of the most remote areas and the loneliest roads in the United States.

Traveling east from Carson City on Highway 50, one can experience the loneliest road in America and several towns along this route with different slogans. These towns were established as Stage Coach Stations or Pony Express stops. One town, Eureka, even bills itself as the "Friendliest Town on the Loneliest Road in America."

A brief look back to Nevada's early history tells much about the present. About the time of the Revolutionary War in America, the Spanish may have become the first set of explorers to enter the Nevada Region. With the next exploration group arriving in 1830 that included Peter Ogden's discovery of the Humboldt River and Jedediah Smith's crossing of southern Nevada, but it was not until the 1840's when John Fremont and Kit Carson explored the Great Basin and Western Nevada that much was known about what is now the State of Nevada. In 1848, the U.S. received Nevada and other lands in the southwest from Mexico with the treaty of "Guadalupe Hidalgo". Congress created Nevada Territory in 1861 and by October 31, 1864 Nevada became the 36th state in the union.

A rich deposit of silver was discovered in 1859 near the present site of Virginia City. Henry Comstock, a prospector, took credit for the find, but others had actually found the ore. This discovery information spread to the fortune hunters in California and back east. Many prospectors came to the Carson County to "Strike it Rich". Almost overnight, Virginia City became a busy mining center, and some miners became very wealthy but many found little wealth for themselves. In the late 1870s the price of silver declined so much that many mines closed and people left Nevada for other states.

In 1931, Nevada passed laws that made gambling legal which led many casinos to start operation during the Depression of the 1930's. In 1927, Nevada passed laws allowing persons to get divorces if they had been a resident for only three months. In 1931, a divorce could be had after only six weeks of residency. These laws caused thousands of persons to come to Nevada to get quick and easy divorces.

The geography of Nevada is reasonable simple. It has some of the Sierra Mountains in the far western part, near Carson City and some of the Columbia Plateau in the northeast corner of the state. Most of Nevada is considered a land region of "Basin and Range." A large part of the Great Basin covers almost the entire state.

The waters of the Great Basin's streams and lakes stay within it. The streams of this basin either dry up or empty into one of the basin's lakes where they evaporate. One unique feature in Nevada is that it has more than twenty mountain ranges running generally north and south in the basin region.

Some must-see areas in Nevada are: the Hoover Dam, Ruth Copper Pit, Lehman Caves and Great Basin National Park. Don't miss the Lake Tahoe area; the cities in that area, Reno, Sparks, and Carson City, are very beautiful. One place that doesn't get mentioned much is Laughlin, in extreme southern Nevada on the Colorado River; this is a true oasis near the Arizona border.

The visitor to Nevada can see much of this state by three Highways: Highway 50, a great experience; Highway 93 up the eastern border to the Idaho Border; and Highway 95 up the western side. There are several ghost towns up to the Oregon border to see. We have traveled in Nevada several times and enjoyed each trip. There is always something to see in this state that will surprise you and catch your interest.

★ Kelly's Perspective & Lessons Learned ★

If you enjoy the water, Lake Mead is the nation's largest man-made reservoir, which is 110 miles long and covers 225 square miles, and has over 500 miles of shoreline.

House boating, skiing, and fishing are all popular escapes at Lake Mead. Anglers will discover the lake is stocked with striped and largemouth bass as well as rainbow trout on a regular basis. Just remember to get your fishing license from either Arizona or Nevada before casting that line.

★ Famous People Born in Nevada ★

Eva Adams director of the U.S. Mint, born in Wonder in 1908.

Ben Alexander the actor, born in Garfield in 1911.

Andre Agassi the tennis player, born in Las Vegas in 1970.

Helen Delich Bentley the newspaperwoman, bron in Ruth in 1923.

Hobart Cavanaugh the actor, born in Virginia City in 1886.

Abby Dalton the actress, born in Las Vegas in 1935.

James A. Gibbons the politician, born in Sparks in 1944.

Jack Kramer the tennis player, born in Las Vegas in 1921.

Paul Laxalt the politician, born in Reno in 1922.

Thelma Pat Nixon the First Lady, born in Ely in 1912.

Lute Pease the cartoonist, born in Winnemucca in 1869.

Edna Purviance the actress, born in Reno in 1895.

Harry M. Reid the politician, born in Searchlight in 1939.

David Derek Stacton the author, born in Minden in 1923.

★ Where Will You Visit? ★

_____

_____

_____

_____

★ What Photos Will You Take? ★

_____

_____

_____

_____

State Capital: Concord

State Flower: Purple Lilac

Population: 1,316,470 (Ranks 42nd, as of 2010 Census)

Land Area: 8,952.65 square miles (Ranks 44th)

Population Density: 147 persons per square mile (Ranks 21st)

★ Arlie's Insight & Highlights ★

New Hampshire, the "Granite state," gets its nickname from the state's large granite deposits. It has an early history like many of the New England States. All of New England has a special history of the struggle of people to get established in a new land. New Hampshire was settled in 1623, soon after the Pilgrims made their famous landing at Plymouth, Massachusetts. The people of this state turned a wilderness into an agricultural society early on, as was necessary for survival. Later, the people used their skills to turn the state's resources to some industrial developments.

The people of New Hampshire have played important roles in the overall history of the United States. New Hampshire was the first of the original thirteen colonies to adopt their own constitution in 1776. Late in 1788, the state became the ninth to ratify the United States Constitution. This act put the U.S. Constitution into effect. From about 1689 on for about 75 years, New Hampshire and much of New England was involved in the "French and Indian War", a war that was off and on for decades. This war was where the Indians were allied with the French to gain control of the area from the British.

The geography of New Hampshire is somewhat complex for a small area of about 9,000 square miles. It includes the White Mountains of the northern one-third of the state, the coastal

lowlands of the southeastern corner, and the large central part of the state known as the "Eastern New England Uplands."

The traveler to New Hampshire has a variety of activities to enjoy, depending on the time of year and the area one visits. The state has a small coastal area, less than fifteen miles, that we did not visit, so I can't speak of it and we were unable to visit the White Mountain area, regrettably.

Some areas billed as great places to visit are: the Merrimack Valley area, the White Mountain Region, the Lakes Area, and the Seacoast Region. Some specific places to see are:

The Cathedral of the Pines, as well as Franklin Pierce Homestead, which is a large two-story house where President Pierce spent his early years. It was built in 1804. Other areas of interest are Daniel Webster's birthplace, near Franklin and Shakers Village, which is Sunapee State Beach and America's Stonehenge.

To travel New Hampshire well, the traveler should have a good Rand McNally Road Atlas and a state visitor's guide. Some of the things we enjoyed about the state of New Hampshire were the beautiful small villages that are typical throughout New England, the farm fields along the countryside and the dairy cattle grazing the meadows. Some areas were so beautiful we just had to stop for photographs.

The two visits we made to New Hampshire were at different times of the year. Early autumn is a favorite because of the changing colors in the countryside.

Before I close, I need to mention one of the most historic events in modern history that happened in New Hampshire. The "Bretton Woods" monetary conference was held here in July, 1944. In that year the United States Government chose the Mount Washington Hotel as the site for a gathering of representatives from 44 countries. The Conference established the World Bank, set the gold standard at $35.00 an ounce and chose the American dollar as the backbone of international exchange. The meeting provided the world with a much needed post war currency stability.

★ Kelly's Perspective & Lessons Learned ★

Best seafood chowder discovered during a visit to the charming Woodstock Inn, Station and Brewery while driving through New Hampshire.

★ Famous People Born in New Hampshire ★

Ralph Adams Cram the architect, born in Hampton Falls in 1863.

Charles Anderson Dana the editor, born in Hinsdale in 1819.

Sam Walter Foss the journalist and poet, born in Candia in 1858.

Daniel Chester French the sculptor, born in Exeter in 1850.

Horace Greeley the journalist and politician, born in Amherst in 1811.

Sarah Josepha Hale the editor, born in Newport in 1788.

John Irving the writer, born in Exeter in 1942.

Franklin Pierce the 14th U.S. president, born in Hillsboro in 1804.

Alan Shepard the astronaut, born in East Derry in 1923.

Daniel Webster the statesman, born in Salisbury in 1782.

★ Where Will You Visit? ★

_____
_____
_____
_____

★ What Photos Will You Take? ★

_____
_____
_____
_____

State Capital: Trenton

State Flower: Purple Violet

Population: 8,791,894 (Ranks 11th, as of 2010 Census)

Land Area: 7,354.2 square miles (Ranks 46th)

Population Density: 1,195 persons per square mile (Ranks 1st)

★ Arlie's Insight & Highlights ★

New Jersey, known as "The Garden State", is located in a way that brings ease to sell its products. The large area between the Delaware River and the Atlantic Ocean is much like a large garden; this area is known as the Atlantic Coastal Plain. The nickname of the state comes from the large number of vegetable farms, orchards and other crops grown over most of New

Jersey. Philadelphia and New York City are huge markets for all types of products in addition to the fruits and vegetables produced in this state. New Jersey is a leader in chemical production and ranks high among producers of metals, machinery and food processing. Almost 90% of New Jersey's people live in urban areas. This large urban population does not mean the state is all hustle and bustle, as there are also many small, quiet towns. A large number of people that live here work in Philadelphia, Trenton, North Eastern New Jersey, and the New York City area. Thousands of New Jerseyans commute by train, busses and autos over all the different bridges and through the Lincoln and Holland tunnels daily.

My experience with the state of New Jersey included the business trips to Princeton, when we flew into Newark and traveled by car on to the Western Electric (AT&T) education center in Princeton, New Jersey as well as trips for personal reasons.

A brief look back at New Jersey's history tells us that the road to statehood has been long and turbulent. Pre-settlement is much like New England and other parts of the east coast that include struggles for the settlers. The Dutch and some Swedes tried settling about 1630, but Indian uprisings prevented permanent settlements until around 1660. The Dutch built the fortified town of Bergen, now part of Jersey City and this was the first permanent white settlement of the region.

The English Military got control of New Jersey and other Dutch possessions in North America in 1664. From about 1700 until the 1760's, Colonial New Jersey was a rural society. Most of the residents were occupied with growing their own food and making permanent homes. During the 1760's, this Colony had approximately 100,000 people and the English King appointed a Colonial Governor. The people elected a Colonial Assembly, but only freeholders who owned property valued at (50 English Pounds) or more could vote.

During the 1760's the English passed several laws that caused much unrest in the Colonies, including New Jersey. Most of these laws set high taxes or restricted colonial trade which caused most of the Colonists to want independence. In 1774, some residents of New Jersey dressed as Indians burned supplies of British Tea at Greenwich; it was called the "Greenwich Tea Burning."

The other big event involving the Tea Supply was in 1773, when the more famous "Boston Tea Party" occurred. These actions symbolized the Colonial opposition to the British taxation policies. In 1775, the Revolutionary War started in Massachusetts and many men from New Jersey joined the Patriots in their fight for their independence.

The Geographic location of New Jersey caused it to be a natural battle ground between New York City and Philadelphia during this struggle for independence. Dozens of battles occurred in New Jersey. Some of the most famous were the Battle of Trenton in 1776, the Battle of Princeton in 1777, and at Monmouth in 1778. At the Battle of Trenton, General Washington made his crossing of the Delaware River on Christmas night and attacked the British by surprise.

New Jersey declared its independence from Great Britain and adopted its first constitution on July 2, 1776. In November of 1778, New Jersey ratified the articles of Confederation, this document was like the pre-constitution of our U.S. Constitution. New Jersey became a state on December 18, 1787, when it ratified the U.S. Constitution. New Jersey was the third state to do so. At the convention of 1787, New Jersey proposed a plan to protect the small states, but the convention adopted the Connecticut plan and the compromise created the present two-house congress.

My travels and experiences in New Jersey have occurred over several years. The early trips to the state were business and education. All the trips to Princeton were to learn the correct regimen of corporate management and they were all very beneficial in exchange of ideas and procedures from others that attended from across the country.

Other travels later in life were for pleasure and exploring the country. We found good roads and access to places in New Jersey were easy. The state has the Garden State Parkway, New Jersey Turnpike and the Atlantic City Expressway which all made for quick access to different parts of the state.

Some spots to visit: Six Flags Great Adventure, Monmouth Race Track, Twin Lights Lighthouse, and Gateway National Recreation area, in addition to Fort Nonsense and other sites near Newark, Elizabeth and Patterson New Jersey. In your visit to New Jersey, there is much to see, take time to enjoy it all. Don't miss Atlantic City. Gamble if you must, but don't expect to win a lot! A must-see area includes the beaches from Cape May all the way north to Ocean City and the board-walk at Atlantic City.

Visit the Garden State and make it a joyful journey.

★ Famous People Born in New Jersey ★

Bud Abbott the comedian, born in Asbury Park in 1895.

Edwin "Buzz" Aldrin the astronaut, born in Montclair in 1930.

Judy Blume the author, born in Elizabeth in 1938.

Jon Bon Jovi the musician, born in Sayreville in 1962.

David Copperfield the magician, born in Metuchen in 1956.

Lou Costello the comedian, born in Paterson in 1906.

Jerry Lewis the comedian and film director, born in Newark in 1926.

Jack Nicholson the actor, born in Neptune City in 1937.

Antonin Scalia the jurist, born in Trenton in 1936.

Norman Schwarzkopf the army general, born in Trenton in 1934.

Frank Sinatra the singer and actor, born in Hoboken in 1915.

Meryl Streep the actress, bron in Summit in 1949.

Dave Thomas the restaurateur, born in Atlantic City in 1932.

Dionne Warwick the actress and singer, born in East Orange in 1940.

★ Where Will You Visit? ★

_____

_____

_____

_____

★ What Photos Will You Take? ★

_____

_____

_____

_____

State Capital: Santa Fe

State Flower: Yucca Flower

Population: 2,059,179 (Ranks 36th, as of 2010 Census)

Land Area: 121,298.2 square miles (Ranks 5th)

Population Density: 17 persons per square mile (Ranks 45th)

★ Arlie's Insight & Highlights ★

New Mexico is a land for the true outdoor person. We have had a myriad of trips and experiences in this state. Over the past several years, we have gone fishing near Red River, hunting near Clayton, skiing at Red River, Angel Fire, Taos and sightseeing throughout the entire state. When we think of the nickname, the "Land of Enchantment," nothing could be

more accurate for the state of New Mexico. It is the fifth largest state in the union, area-wise. It has a wide variety of terrain that includes the Great Plains over the eastern one third, while the central and southwest is considered a basin and range region. The north central is Rocky Mountains and northwest is part of the Colorado Plateau. The state is mainly dry overall, but parts of the "High Country" receive considerable snowfall, making beautiful ski country in winter months.

New Mexico claims the oldest road in the U.S., the El Camino Real (The Royal Road). It was a 1600 mile road from Mexico City to the San Juan Pueblo near present site of Santa Fe, New Mexico. There are many historic sites of interest in this state, but be prepared to travel several hundred miles in this very large land.

When we speak of early history in the United States, we must include New Mexico. The colorful past and the fact that Indian ruins still standing that had as many as 800 rooms in one building, is testimony to the Native Indians that lived here hundreds of years before Columbus ever discovered America. Spain ruled what is now New Mexico for more than 250 years and the oldest seat of their government was in Santa Fe as early as 1610. Santa Fe remains as the present Capital of New Mexico today.

As late as 1680, the Pueblo Indians drove the Spanish out of what is northern New Mexico, but the Spanish re-took the area by 1692. In 1821, New Mexico became a province of Mexico and William Becknell, a trader, opened the Santa Fe Trail when he bought the first goods down from Missouri. The stage coach service followed in 1849 from Independence Missouri.

In 1846, General Kearney took possession of New Mexico during the war with Mexico and in 1848; Mexico ceded New Mexico to the U.S. in the treaty of Guadalupe Hidalgo. Two years later, Congress created the Territory of New Mexico. By 1853, the area of present New Mexico was complete with the Gadsden Purchase.

The 1860's and 1870's were a turbulent time in New Mexico. In1864, Kit Carson defeated the Mescalero Apache and Navajo Indians and by 1876 the cattlemen in the area became involved in what is known as the Lincoln County War. Billy the Kid and other outlaws took a leading part in the fighting of this war. Geronimo, was one of the last hostile Apache Chiefs to surrender terrorized the area for a time before he surrendered in September of 1886.

Modern day New Mexico is much settled and a great place to visit. The World's first atomic bomb was set-off on July 16, 1945, near Alamogordo, but was assembled at Los Alamos. It seems every visit to the state of New Mexico, we discover something new and interesting. Some of the most exciting times we have enjoyed was in the Angel Fire, Red River and Taos area skiing and learning to ski. Some of the clearest memories are when we practicing at Taos, side stepping the mountain all day and when we could take the ski lift, we were too tired to do so. The hot tub was a much better option! The cross-country skiing at Red River was also great fun for us; these adventures are special moments that will be in our memories forever.

The three hunting trips to eastern New Mexico for me were all rewarding. I hunted around Santa Rosa and near Springer, great for early fall. The trout fishing is best in north central and northwest New Mexico.

Some great places to visit and things to see: in the northwestern part: Aztec Ruins National Monument, Angel Peak National Recreation Area, and the Four Corners area. In southwestern part: Steins Ghost Town and Shakespeare Ghost Town as well as Gila Cliff Dwellings National Monument. In south central part: White Sands Space Harbor and Lincoln St. Monument. In the central part from Socorro to Albuquerque are several old Spanish Missions. In the North Central one will find Bandelier National Monument, Ft. Union National Monument, Philmont National Boy Scout Ranch, and the Capulin Volcano National Monument at Capulin.

A trek to and across New Mexico for fishing, hunting, sightseeing or hiking, is sure to be rewarding; we have done all of them. Enjoy this journey.

★ Kelly's Perspective & Lessons Learned ★

Growing up, I remember several road trips through New Mexico and exploring towns of all shapes and sizes with my parents.

In some cases those destinations had remarkable histories, although very little of the population remained.

As proof, my mom captured a childhood photo of me and my Dad in Elizabethtown, which is mostly a ghost town now. The photo is a favorite, that my Dad had in his collection and that we included in this chapter.

★ Famous People Born in New Mexico ★

Bruce Cabot the actor, born in Carlsbad in 1904.

Dennis Chavez the senator, born in Los Chavez 1888.

Mangas Coloradas the Apache leader, born in 1793.

Robert Crichton the author, born in Albuquerque in 1925.

John Denver the singer, born in Roswell in 1943.

Pete Domenici the senator, born in Albuquerque in 1932.

Sid Gutierrez the astronaut, born in Albuquerque in 1951.

William Hanna the animator, born in Melrose in 1910.

Neil Patrick Harris the actor, born in Albuquerque in 1973.

Demi Moore the actress, born in Roswell in 1962.

Al Unser the auto racer, born in Albuquerque in 1939.

Bobby Unser the auto racer, born in Albuquerque in 1934.
Victorio the Apache chief, born about 1825.

★ Where Will You Visit? ★

★ What Photos Will You Take? ★

State Capital: Albany

State Flower: Rose

Population: 19,378,102 (Ranks 3rd, as of 2010 Census)

Land Area: 47,126.4 square miles (Ranks 30th)

Population Density: 411.2 persons per square mile (Ranks 7th)

★ Arlie's Insight & Highlights ★

New York is truly the "Empire State;" it is by definition an extensive enterprise maintained by a unified authority. This state is diverse with mountains, flat lands, very large cities and many small towns. While many people think of New York City when they hear about New York, the city does not define this entire state. I have visited this state many times and have enjoyed it all. Upstate New York is much like most parts of New England: it is beautiful with rivers, lakes and many mountains. Every visitor should make a point to see what many of us call "Up-State" New York.

It's difficult to express how important New York City is to the U.S. economy and the world economy as a whole. It is one of the nation's leading centers for business, banking, culture and manufacturing. New York City is considered the cultural center of the Western Hemisphere; it has one of the world's busiest seaports and in the harbor we find the Statue of Liberty which has been a symbol of freedom for people from all parts of the world. Nearby in the harbor is Ellis Island where millions of persons passed through before it closed in 1954. There is so much to see in New York City that it takes several days to tour and observe part of this community. We know because we did it, with a specific plan to see as much of this giant city as possible on this special occasion.

New York City consists of five boroughs, all of which have large populations. They are: The Bronx, Queens, Brooklyn, Staten Island, and Manhattan. Most of them are separated by rivers but there are bridges and tunnels that facilitate travel among the different parts. Some of the major ones are: The Holland Tunnel, The Lincoln Tunnel, Brooklyn Bridge, Manhattan Bridge, Williamsburg Bridge, Queensboro Bridge, George Washington Bridge and Queens Tunnel. Most of the sights, banking, theaters and fun things are found in Manhattan, including Central Park. River tours and the trip out to the Statue of Liberty National Monument are must-see sights. Take plenty of time and tour all of Manhattan: Battery Park, U.N. Headquarters, Theater District, Garment District, Central Park and please don't miss the great museums.

The first people to live in the New York City area were Ameri-

can Indians who lived along the Hudson and East Rivers. The Indians fished, hunted, trapped animals, and raised crops. The first European to enter the area was Verrazano, an Italian explorer working for the King of France. He and his crew landed on Staten Island in 1524, while exploring the east coast of North America, however no settlement occurred. Finally, in 1609, Henry Hudson arrived at Manhattan and explored this river that now bears the name Hudson. Hudson was an Englishman working for the Dutch, so they claimed this land for the Netherlands.

In 1613, a Dutch Trader and his crew became the first Europeans to live on Manhattan Island. In 1624, the Dutch West India Co., a colonizing firm sent the first settlers to Manhattan Island and by 1626, those settlers had built a fort named Fort Amsterdam on Manhattan. During this same year Governor Peter Minuit bought the island from the Native Americans for goods worth the equivalent of about $24 dollars. The Dutch and English fought three naval battles from 1652 and 1674 for control of the area, but in 1664 the English forced the Dutch to surrender New Amsterdam. The Dutch regained the colony a few years later, but had to give it back to the English under terms of a peace treaty. This time the English renamed the colony New York.

During the Revolutionary War, New York played a great role in helping the colonists fight for freedom from Great Britain. In 1775, American forces took possession of New York City, but the British regained the city after the Battle of Long Island in 1776 and they kept it until the war ended in 1783. However, in January of 1785, New York became the temporary capital of the new United States of America. Congress met in New York in March of 1789 and General George Washington was inaugurated as our Nation's First President in April of 1789.

New York State and New York City have a rich and turbulent history, but in 1776, New York approved the Declaration of Independence and on July 26, 1788, New York became the 11th state in the union.

Another "Red Letter Day" for New York was the Erie Canal opening in 1825, which linked the Hudson River and the Great Lakes. Another special day in history was the United Nations Headquarters being completed, in 1952, in New York City.

The visitor to New York State, should make a plan, get good maps and a visitor's guide for the state, as well as take a camera to capture the special scenes, such as Niagara Falls, which is a must-see for any traveler to this part of New York and the surrounding area.

If the visitor travels from Buffalo, New York east on Interstate 90, there are many great side trips to other large beautiful cit-

ies, beginning with Rochester on Lake Ontario, Syracuse, and the Utica-Rome area. One great side trip is from Amsterdam north into the Adirondack Mountains. The first site visitors see is a large beautiful lake, Great Scandaga Lake, at the southern edge of the mountains. From this southern tip of the Adirondacks, all the way north to Lake Placid and beyond, one can see many lakes, rivers, old forts, ski areas and many recreational sites that are not found in other parts of the country.

If one travels on east to Schenectady, they will be near Troy and Albany, which is the State Capital of New York. All of upstate New York is very scenic and to travel this area is a pleasure for the adventurous soul.

★ Kelly's Perspective & Lessons Learned ★

With focus on New York City, favorite itineraries have included: touring the Metropolitan Museum with a break for lunch if possible, any meal at Sarabeth's in the upper west or east side, a day time carriage ride through Central Park, a morning tour of Wall Street, lunch on Staten Island (travel via the free ferry) and wrap up the day in the heart of Times Square to enjoy the theater district or one of many fine dining establishments. These are the first seven opportunities

to experience the city (that come to mind) with the understanding that dozens of other sites, activities, and happenings are available in the city that never sleeps.

★ Famous People Born in New York ★

Kareem Abdul-Jabbar the basketball player, born in New York City in 1947.

Lucille Ball the actress, born in Jamestown in 1911.

Humphrey Bogart the actor, born in New York City in 1899.

Sammy Davis, Jr. the actor and singer, born in New York City in 1925.

Henry Louis Gehrig baseball player, born in Yorkville in 1903.

Jackie Gleason the comedian and actor, born in Brooklyn in 1916

Michael Jeffery Jordan the basketball player, born in Brooklyn in 1963.

Vince Lombardi the football coach, born in Brooklyn in 1913.

The Marx Brothers, Chico (1897), Harpo (1888), Groucho (1890), and Zeppo (1901) the comedians, all born in New York City.

John D. Rockefeller the industrialist, born in Richford in 1839.

Norman Rockwell painter and illustrator, born in New York City in 1894.

Mickey Rooney the actor, born in Brooklyn in 1920.

Franklin D. Roosevelt the 32nd U.S. president, born in Hyde Park in 1882.

Barbra Streisand singer and actress, born in New York City in 1942.

★ Where Will You Visit? ★

_____
_____
_____
_____

★ What Photos Will You Take? ★

_____
_____
_____
_____

State Capital: Raleigh

State Flower: Flowering Dogwood

Population: 9,535,483 (Ranks 29th, as of 2010 Census)

Land Area: 48,617.9 square miles (Ranks 29th)

Population Density: 196.1 persons per square mile (Ranks 15th)

★ Arlie's Insight & Highlights ★

North Carolina, known also as the "Tar Heel State", is a state of unusual beauty. My memories of North Carolina standout as a place of the Blue Ridge Mountains, large areas of azaleas, and places to enjoy plenty of the early history of our country.

North Carolina acquired its nickname when the state's troops were fighting during the Civil War. The Confederate Troops fighting on the same side decided to retreat, leaving the North

Carolina Troops to fight it out alone. Later, the North Carolinians threatened to put tar on the heels of the other confederate troops so they would stick to the fight and not retreat.

North Carolina holds a lot of mystery in the early attempts to settle the area. Sir Walter Raleigh from England made a move to settle on Roanoke Island in 1585. This group was the first of the English colonists in America. Some attempts were made earlier by the French and Spanish who were exploring the east coast of North America. The first was an Italian, Verrazano, exploring in the service of France sometime in 1524, where he visited the Cape Fear area. About two years later, a Spanish Colony was established near Cape Fear, but disease and hunger killed many and the survivors left this area. By 1540, Hernando De Soto from Spain led an expedition over what is North Carolina, looking for gold. De Soto went all the way to the Mississippi River in 1541. But neither the Spanish nor the French made any permanent settlements.

Sir Walter Raleigh did persevere. He later sent an expedition to Roanoke Island in 1587, with Mr. John White as Governor. He established a colony and went back to England for additional supplies for the year. When the Queen of England allowed White to return to Roanoke Island in 1590, the entire colony has disappeared. To this day, the mystery remains as to what happened to this settlement of more than a hundred men, women and children. It is known as the "Lost Colony of Roanoke". The first white settlers came from Virginia and settled in the Albemarle area about 1650. Some years later in the late 1600's, the region of Carolina was divided into what is North and South Carolina, but it was not until 1712 when North Carolina became a separate Colony.

A turbulent time occurred in the early 1700's for North Carolina. This was a period known as the "Colonial Wars." North Carolina helped England fight several of these wars. From 1739 to 1744, they fought against the Spaniards in what is now Georgia. Other wars were The Queen Ann's War from 1702 until 1713, King George's War from 1744 until 1748, and lasting for many years, the French and Indian War, from 1754 to 1763. Finally, the war with the Cherokee Indians ended with a peace treaty in 1761 and this opened up large areas for settlement in the Carolinas.

The Revolutionary War period was also a turbulent time for North Carolina. Even though most of the War was fought outside of North Carolina, the people of North Carolina joined the fight against Great Britain. Those who opposed the British were called "Whigs" and those who remained loyal to the British were called "Tories." In 1780, British troops led by Lord Cornwallis marched on North Carolina from the south but were defeated. Then Cornwallis attacked again and got into the state, but on March 15, 1781, General Greene's Colonial

Forces beat Cornwallis' troops in battle and the British abandoned the state of North Carolina.

After the Revolutionary War ended and the "Bill of Rights" was added to the Constitution, North Carolina finally ratified the Constitution in November of 1789.

The Civil War was a struggle for North Carolina. It tried to preserve the union even after most southern states had seceded from the union. After the war started on April 12, 1861, North Carolina finally supplied 125,000 men to the Confederate cause. The Civil War caused many deaths, despair, and destruction to North Carolina. Plantations were divided into small farms, which doubled the number of them between 1860 & 1880. Tobacco became the main crop and factories were built to process it. In addition, the furniture industry and cotton processing also flourished on a large-scale.

For the visitor, North Carolina has much to offer. Regrettably we have not visited all the east coast of this state, but the part we visited was very beautiful and enjoyable. There is enough early history on the coast to keep a visitor moving around for several days of travel, this may call for a return trip someday.

The area around Asheville, Waynesville, and the Great Smoky Mountains National Park are must-sees for any visitor to North Carolina. The Biltmore Estate is one-of-a-kind experience; this French Renaissance Chateau Home is billed as the largest house in America (178,926 sq. ft.). The winery and gardens are awesome. Visit this place on a guided tour and you will have seen the most lavish house of all, built during the peak of the "Gilded Age". There is other scenery in the Blue Ridge Mountains and Mount Mitchell, as well as many lakes and rivers to view.

As one travels east of the mountains in the state, you will experience the great Piedmont region and then the Atlantic Coastal Plains Region where all the great tobacco, soybean, corn, fruits, and other crops are grown.

North Carolina is one place I would like to visit again, especially part of the east coast from Cape Lookout North, to the Virginia Line. There appears to be lots of interesting history here for me.

Like many Americans, I will always be intrigued about the "Lost Colony of Roanoke Island" and what really happened to the 90 men, 17 women and 11 children that disappeared without a trace. I have read some of the theories, but it appears we will have to accept what happened without knowing the details.

★ Famous People Born in North Carolina ★

Howard Cosell the sportscaster, born in Winston-Salem in 1918.

Elizabeth Hanford Dole the public official, born in Salisbury in 1936.

Roberta Flack the singer, born in Black Mountain in 1937.

Ava Gardner the actress, born in Smithfield in 1922.

Billy Graham the evangelist, born in Charlotte in 1918.

Andy Griffith the actor, born in Mount Airy in 1926.

Jesse Helms the politician, born in Monroe in 1921.

O. Henry the writer, born in Greensboro in 1862.

Andrew Johnson the 17th U.S. president, born in Raleigh in 1808.

Charles Kuralt the TV journalist, born in Wilmington in 1934.

Richard Petty the auto racer, born in Level Cross in 1937.

James K. Polk the 11th U.S. president, born in Mechlenburg in 1795.

Soupy Sales the comedian, born in Wake Forest in 1926.

Earl Scruggs the bluegrass musician, born in Flint Hill in 1924.

Randy Travis the musician, born in Charlotte in 1959.

★ Where Will You Visit? ★

★ What Photos Will You Take? ★

State Capital: Bismarck

State Flower: Wild Prairie Rose

Population: 672,591 (Ranks 48th, as of 2010 Census)

Land Area: 69,000.9 square miles (Ranks 17th)

Population Density: 9.7 persons per square mile (Ranks 47th)

★ Arlie's Insight & Highlights ★

North Dakota's nicknamed the Flickertail State, because of the numerous amount of Flickertail, ground squirrels that live there. The Sioux Indians also called themselves, "Dakota" meaning allies or friends. My memories that stand-out, traveling the western part of this state, was the difficulty of getting a room at night because of the oil boom. Oil has quickly become the state's most valuable industry.

It was late one evening, (10 P.M.) and we were tired from traveling all day, so we stopped at the best new motel in town and ask the clerk for a room. She replied, "we are full-up, the oil boom keeps us with no vacancy". I said, "thank you", but I will leave this $50.00 bill with you and we will be eating dinner at that restaurant across the street. We were half-way through our meal, when a lady walked in and said to us I think we have a room for you, I said, "Great", we'll take it.

My wife had ask me at the start of our dinner meal, where will we be sleeping tonight? I told her we would be sleeping in the Motel we had just departed. It turned out the Motel had moved one of the oil company's employees to a room that was pre-paid, but not occupied; we were fortunate once again!

North Dakota, is mainly a farming state, but the oil production has had more press in recent years. The main crop is wheat, however, other important crops are flaxseed, barley and rye In total, the farm region stretches from the Red River in the east to the western border.

Looking back on the history of North Dakota, one can see it was slow to settle, roads were poor or non-existing, but the main reason little settlement occurred before 1870 was that settlers were fearful of Indian attacks. The number of residents included approximately 2500 persons in 1870, and only 20 years later in 1890, the number had grown to more than 190,000 persons.

North Dakota was first explored, by a French Canadian, who came down from Canada in 1738, and came as far as the present day Bismarck area near the Mandan Indian Villages at that time. In 1762, France gave its land west of the Mississippi to Spain. Spain, later gave it back to France in 1800, and in 1803, the U.S. purchased it from France. Lewis and Clark, on their mission to explore a route to the Pacific Ocean, built Fort Mandan on the east bank of the Missouri River in 1804 and in April of 1805, they passed on their way to the Pacific Ocean and came back through this route in 1806.

In February, of 1889, Congress established the current boundaries, between North Dakota and South Dakota. It also set up an act allowing these two regions to have the means to become states. On November 2, 1889, North Dakota became the 39th state and South Dakota, became the 40th state in the union. North Dakota grew rapidly after statehood, and by 1910 the population had grown to more than 570.000 persons and farming grew at a rapid pace.

For the western history buff, there is much to see across North Dakota. On the east side, one will find; Fort Ransom, near Lisbon, Maple Creek Historic Site, near Leonard, Fort Abercrombie, near Mooreton, Pembina Settlement, near Pembina and Fort Totten History Site, near Fort Totten.

Near Bismarck, is Mandan Earth Lodges, which are dome-shaped, that have been restored, it is called Slant Village. Fort Mandan Historic site and Fort Clark, near Washburn. On the west side of the state, one can find several places of interest to the visitor.

Beginning in the southwest corner is; Fort Dilts Historic Site, near Rhames. Theodore Roosevelt National Park, south unit at Belfield, Theodore Roosevelt National Park (Elk Horn Ranch), Killdeer Battlefield site, near Killdeer. Near Williston, is the Fort Union Trading Post and Fort Buford State Historic site.

If you enjoy the farm and ranch country of the great plains, you will enjoy western North Dakota. The Red River Valley of eastern North Dakota is a great area for farm crops, while the center and northern portion is hilly ranch country.

The "Geographic center of North America", is found near Rugby. Traveling through North Dakota is pleasant and easy, but if you travel in the Williston Basin area, please call ahead for reservations!

★ Famous People Born in North Dakota ★

Elizabeth Bodine the humanitarian, born in Velva in 1898.

Angie Dickinson the actress, born in Kulm in 1931.

Rev. Richard C. Halverson the U.S. Senate chaplain, born in Pingree in 1916.

Louis L'Amour the author, born in Jamestown in 1908.

Peggy Lee the singer, born in Jamestown in 1920.

Cliff Fido Purpur the hockey player and coach, born in Grand Forks in 1914.

James Rosenquist the painter, born in Grand Forks in 1933.

Eric Sevareid the TV commentator, born in Velva in 1912.

Ann Sothern the actress, born in Valley City in 1909.

Tommy Tucker the band leader, born in Souris in 1933.

Lawrence Welk the band leader and entertainer, born in Strasburg in 1903.

★ Where Will You Visit? ★

★ What Photos Will You Take? ★

State Capital: Columbus

State Flower: Scarlet Carnation

Population: 11,536,504 (Ranks 7th, as of 2010 Census)

Land Area: 40,860.69 square miles (Ranks 35th)

Population Density: 282.3 persons per square mile (Ranks 10th)

★ Arlie's Insight & Highlights ★

Ohio "The Buckeye State" is a stand-out in history. I recall three major city tours we took over time that were most interesting. I will start with Cincinnati, the City on the River, sometimes called the "City of Seven Hills." The setting of Cincinnati is somewhat unique, in that the best view for the town is from the Ohio River. One day we took a cruise up-river and had a great visit with two Amish families from out-of-town. These hard-working people appear to lead simple lives and avoid modern ways. We asked how they arrived at the river and they told us they jointly hired a private van to travel from the farms to the river location. Most of the women wore the full-skirted dresses and some wore bonnets while most of the men had beards. They said, "all the family's clothing was homemade" and that their "People" had lived in Ohio since the mid 1800's. We had a great visit with these families, including the children.

After spending some time in the Cincinnati area, we journeyed to Columbus, where we toured this city and the surrounding area's places of interest to us. The zoo was of special interest and several of the old historic sites around town. Columbus is one of those cities that are rich in history and heritage. There are more than 300 properties listed on the National Register in Franklin County.

From my brochures and memories, I recall some of those places in the Columbus area; the Richard Berry House, the James Thurber House, the Jonathan Noble House, the Drake House and the Jones Mansion. The "Mounds', remains from the Mound Builders (Indians) are always present in many parts of Ohio, this is also true of the Columbus area.

Our visit to the Cleveland area, on the Great Lakes Plains was still much different than other areas of Ohio. The Lake Erie shores are where a wide variety of crops, especially fruit and vegetables are grown in this fertile soil. The region in and around Cleveland includes a great deal of manufacturing, lake ports and shipping. To state accurately, it is a heavily populated and busy area of Ohio. No visit to Cleveland would be complete without a cruise on Lake Erie, also, a visit to the "Rock and Roll Hall of Fame and Museum" on the shore of Lake Erie; this is downtown Cleveland and part of "North Coast Harbor" complex. There are plenty of great sights from the Cleveland area all the way west along the lake to Toledo, a trip of about 100 miles.

There are too many historic sites and other places of interest in Ohio to list them separately, but I will list a few on the eastern side of Ohio: from Canton are the Pro Football Hall of Fame, Ft. Laurens and Zoar Village State Memorials, near Zoar, White Woman's Rock and Roscoe Village, near Coshocton.

Ohio is blessed by being the birthplace of seven Presidents of the United States, it is only exceeded by Virginia, the state of the birth place of eight Presidents. In Ohio, listed in order of their term of their Presidency; Ulysses Grant (18), Rutherford Hayes (19), James Garfield (20), Benjamin Harrison (23), William McKinley (25), William Taft (27) and Warren Harding (29). All of these Presidents have historic sites in Ohio. Some other places of interest in Northern Ohio are: Perry's Victory and International Peace Memorial at Put-In-Bay and Glacial Grooves St. Memorial nearby, at Cedar Point at Sandusky and Fallen Timbers Memorial, near Toledo. Some places in western Ohio are; Fort Defiance Memorial at Defiance, Indian Trail Caverns, Ghost Town and Hull Old Trail Monument at Findlay. In central Ohio visitors will find: Mound Builders St. Memorial at Newark and Flint Ridge St. Memorial at Gratiot, Seip Mound St. Monument at Bainbridge, and Temper Mound at Portsmouth.

A brief look back at Ohio's early history, we discovered that the French had a great influence in the area. About 1670, a French explorer, Robert Cavelier De La Salle is probably the first white man to arrive in what is now Ohio. The French based their claim to the entire northwest on this visit and exploration by La Salle. But the British claimed all the land (territory) inland from their Atlantic colonies.

This dispute between the French and British over Territory in North America, including Ohio, led to the 9 year French and Indian War, from 1754 to 1763. The Peace Treaty of 1763, gave the British most of the lands east of the Mississippi River. In

1780, George Clark defeated the Indian allies of the British in the battle of Piqua. Clark's campaign in the northwest helped win this region for the U.S. during the Revolutionary War. The northwest ordinance of 1787, made way for the statehood of Ohio and other divisions of this territory. In April of 1788, the Ohio Company founded Marietta, the first permanent white settlement in Ohio. Marietta became the first capital of the northwest territory, in 1788. A short time later, several communities developed along the Ohio River. Many of these settlers were war veterans who received land in payment for their duty in the Revolution War service.

In 1800, Congress passed the Division Act, this created the Indiana Territory out of the western part of northwestern territory. Preparation for Ohio's statehood started in November, 1802, and Ohio became the 17th state in the union on March 1, 1803.

The geography of Ohio consist of three main regions, The Great Lakes Plains, all along the northern border, the Till Plains cover much of central and western Ohio and the Appalachian Plateau covers almost half of this state's east and south eastern side.

Before visiting Ohio, be sure to acquire some good maps of cities and a visitor's guide to locate some of the primary attractions. I will list some of those the traveler may find interesting, outside the major cities of Ohio; Zoar Village, near new Philadelphia, founded in 1817, the National Pro football Hall of Fame, in Canton, Adena State Memorial, in Chillicothe, a stone house built in 1807, the Campus Martius Museum, in Marietta, a State Memorial, Fort Recovery, a reproduction of part of the fort built in 1793, used during the Indian Wars.

There are many Indian mounds and other historic structures; Fort Ancient, near Lebanon, is the largest hilltop earth structure in the U.S. The "Great Serpent Mound", near Hillsboro is one of the best-known pre-historic structures in the world. The mound, shaped like a snake, has seven curves!

There are many interesting things to see in this state, take your time and enjoy the history of Ohio.

★ Kelly's Perspective & Lessons Learned ★

Having lived in Ohio, the first three things that come to mind are: dear friends, Hyde Park, and Graeter's Ice Cream.

Many friends remain in the greater Cincinnati area and I will plan a return visit. Regarding the neighborhoods, I chose Hyde Park (est. 1892) to live in because of the historic charm, location, and the cottage that I fell in love with, which is pictured in this chapter. Another benefit of residing in the neighborhood

was the close proximity of the Graeter's Ice Cream parlor that has been present on the Hyde Park Square since 1938.

★ Famous People Born in Ohio ★

Neil Alden Armstrong the astronaut, born in Wapakoneta in 1930.

Ambrose Bierce the journalist, born in Meigs County in 1842.

Erma Bombeck the columnist and humorist, born in Dayton in 1927.

Bill "Hopalong Cassidy" Boyd the actor, born in Cambridge in 1895.

William Jennings Bryan the U.S. presidential candidate, born in Salem in 1860.

Milton Caniff the cartoonist, born in Hillsboro in 1907.

Nancy Cartwright the voice of Bart Simpson, born in Kettering in 1957.

Dorothy Dandridge the actress, born in Cleveland in 1922.

Doris Day the singer and actress, born in Cincinnati in 1924.

Clarence Seward Darrow the lawyer, born in Kingsman in 1857.

Hugh Downs the TV broadcaster, born in Akron in 1921.

Thomas Alva Edison the inventor, born in Milan in 1847.

Clark Gable the actor, born in Cadiz in 1901.

James Abram Garfield the 20th U.S. president, born in Cuyahoga County in 1831.

John Herschel Glenn the astronaut and senator, born in Cambridge in 1921.

Ulysses Simpson Grant the 18th U.S. president, born in Point Pleasant in 1822.

Zane Grey the author, born in Zanesville in 1872.

Warren Gamaliel Harding the 29th U.S. president, born in Morrow County in 1865.

Rutherford Hayes the 19th U.S. president, born in Delaware in 1822.

Benjamin Harrison the 23rd U.S. president, born in North Bend in 1833.

Robert Henri the painter, born in Cincinnati in 1865.

Dean Martin the singer and actor, born in Steubenville in 1917.

William McKinley the 25th U.S. president, born in Niles in 1843.

Paul Newman the actor, born in Cleveland in 1925.

Jack Nicklaus the golfer, born in Columbus in 1940.

Annie Oakley the markswoman, born in Darke County in 1860.

Norman Vincent Peale the clergyman, born in Bowersville in 1898.

Tyrone Power the actor, born in Cincinnati in 1914.

Judith Resnik the astronaut, born in Akron in 1949.

William Tecumseh Sherman the army general, born in Lancaster in 1820.

Steven Spielberg the director and screenwriter, born in Cincinnati in 1946.

Gloria Steinem the feminist, born in Toledo in 1934.

William H. Taft the 27th U.S. president, born in Cincinnati in 1857.

Ted Turner the broadcasting mogul, born in Cincinnati in 1938.

Orville Wright the inventor, born in Dayton in 1871.

Cy Young the baseball player, born in Gilmore in 1867.

★ Where Will You Visit? ★

★ What Photos Will You Take? ★

State Capital: Oklahoma City

State Flower: Mistletoe

Population: 3,751,351 (Ranks 28th, as of 2010 Census)

Land Area: 68,594.2 square miles (Ranks 19th)

Population Density: 54.7 persons per square mile (35th)

★ Arlie's Insight & Highlights ★

Oklahoma is known as the 'Sooner State', as a result of its rich heritage. A heritage, that brought many adventurous individuals to Oklahoma starting in the late 1800's. It appears that same spirit resides in their offspring, who manage ranches and farms throughout the state.

Before we go on, it is appropriate to take a look at the esteemed state history. In the 1820's the Federal Government identified a place for the Five Civilized Tribes to settle, as they had been displaced from their homeland in the east. These tribes included: Chickasaw, Choctaw, Cherokee, Creek, and Seminole. These five tribes were assigned land in the eastern part of Oklahoma. This move to Oklahoma was very difficult and described by some of the Tribes as "The Trail of Tears." The U.S. Government promised to protect the tribes and guaranteed the Native Americans would own the land "…as long as grass grows and rivers run."

These treaties and promises were torn apart by The Civil War (1860 – 1865). During the late 1860's, many of the cattlemen from Texas crossed the Native American lands with their herds to the rail stations in Kansas. Some cattle owners paid their toll and some did not – despite an estimated 6 million cattle crossing this land from 1866 to 1885. The main passageways were the Chisholm Trail, the Shawnee and the Great Western Trails.

In 1885, the Cattlemen's Association, attempting to restore order, leased approximately 6 million acres from the Indians for 5 years. However, the Government declared the leases invalid.

Later in 1890, President Harrison ordered all white men to remove their cattle from the area. The group known as the 'Boomers' urged the Government to open the land for settlement. Finally, urging worked and 3 million acres were purchased from the Creek and Seminole Tribes.

The portion left open to settlement was more than half of the total purchased. It was to be opened for settlement at noon on April 22, 1889. People were so anxious to settle this fertile land, it was necessary to have the Army physically present to hold them back. The result: Two memorable towns were settled that day – Guthrie and Oklahoma City, with approximately 10,000 people in each city.

As a precursor, some settlers called "Sooners" went into the area early to claim some of the best land. These "Sooners" actually got away with their actions by rather devious means.

Taking a look back in history, my 1890 *Rand McNally Atlas* shows Oklahoma to be split into two parts: Oklahoma Territory and Indian Territory. Interestingly, the Indian Territory was largely the remaining land of the Five Civilized Tribes. However, these Tribes were only part of the Indian population in what is now Oklahoma.

In what is now western Oklahoma, several tribes known as the Plains Indians were present. These tribes included: Comanche, Cheyenne, Caddos, Arapahos, Kiowas, Osage, Wichita, and Pawnees, with some other lesser-known tribes. Most of the Plains Indians had followed huge herds of buffalo that grazed on grassy prairies. After the buffalo disappeared, many of these tribes settled in parts of Oklahoma to farm and take on other activities; these adjustments were difficult, but appeared to have worked out over time.

If one looked at a map of Oklahoma today, it is easy to see that a City, Town, or County has been named for each of these Tribes.

By May 1890, Congress had established Oklahoma as a Territory, with Guthrie as the Capital. In 1893, a Great Land Run, known as the "Cherokee Outlet", opened up in North-Central Oklahoma. This was the Tonkawa and Pawnee Reservations, about 6 million acres were claimed on Sept 16, 1893.

Progress toward Statehood evolved over the next several years and Congress insisted the two Territories become one territory to form the great State of Oklahoma and on November 16, 1907 Oklahoma became the 46th State in the union.

I will explain later why the extensive background (history) was necessary and the number of the Native Americans (e.g., Indians) living in the State was spotlighted. Building on that, it's not only the cities, towns, and counties that have Indian names but the name Oklahoma comes from two Choctaw Indian words: Okla = People and Homa = Red.

From here, we fast forward to the 1930's. This decade was tough and very challenging for the people of Oklahoma. The Great Depression of the 30's left a path of devastation across the state and the "Dust Bowl" era emerged. The Dust Bowl was felt in the western part of the State more than the eastern portion. Combined together, the Great Depression and the Dust Bowl caused the State to lose a large number of residents.

John Steinbeck's book, *The Grapes Of Wrath*, tells the story of how poor farmers of Oklahoma migrated to California and were mistreated by others while experiencing great hardships. At the time, the term 'Okie' was attached to those migrating out of the state and to other regions. This stigma would carry over for many years as the region slowly recovered.

In the decades that followed World War II to 1970, Oklahoma increased soil conservation and farming practices to help restore much of the land that eroded during the 1930's. As a result new dams and lakes were built to leverage the rainfall across the state, especially in eastern Oklahoma.

Today the state has barge traffic near Tulsa and at Muskogee from the Arkansas River, that connects with the Mississippi River System. These waterways allow grains and other materials to

be shipped to various destinations within the state.

Further, a number of recreation areas are in the eastern half of Oklahoma, where one can find more than a dozen large lakes. Some of them are 50,000 acres or larger. In addition, Oklahoma has more than two dozen State Parks.

Another piece of history that has been part of Oklahoma, since 1926, and includes the main street of America, "Old Route 66", which has both a hit song and television series named after it. Also known as the 'Mother Road', more than 150 miles of it can still be traveled on an intermittent basis. This is a road that I have known well as I was born and raised near it.

Museums and other places to visit in the state include: the National Cowboy Hall of Fame, the Western Heritage Center, and the Woolaroc Museum which showcases works from Charles Russell, Frederic Remington and other distinguished artists.

In and around Tulsa, the Thomas Gilcrease Museum setting on 460 acres, houses the world's largest collection of art and artifacts of the American west. The Will Rogers Memorial in Claremore is worth visiting and holds exhibits of both Will Rogers and early pioneers of Oklahoma.

Along with four full seasons, Oklahoma has many activities that celebrate changes in flora and temperature including: Muskogee's Azalea Festival (April/May); Porter's Peach Festival plus the Rush Springs Watermelon Festival (August); and as the leafs turn, Yukon's Czech Festival takes place in my neighborhood (October).

Another activity that draws national coverage in the fall and winter is Oklahoma's football season. Both Oklahoma University (OU) and Oklahoma State University (OSU) continue to capture national titles and have devoted fans in our own family. The devotion brings those fans, (my children) great distances to visit us and attend games.

As our travels and the family vacations continue, so do our stories. One that ties back to our state's rich heritage reminds me of a conversation that took place in Buffalo, New York a few years back. We were with fellow travelers in a hotel lobby and a woman overheard that I was visiting from Oklahoma. After learning this, she asked me if it was still safe to travel across the state without being attacked by Indians. I assured her, with a big smile that Oklahoma's stage coaches were much safer and we both had a good laugh!

★ Kelly's Perspective & Lessons Learned ★

Being born and raised in Oklahoma allowed me to grow up appreciating family, friends, animals, nature, and certainly football.

It would be easy to write several chapters on all of the mentors (and occasional tormentors) that shaped my early years in Oklahoma. Maybe that will be the inspiration for a future book? Until then, my most important lesson: Remember to be yourself. In a world that is constantly trying to make you something else, being yourself, is the greatest accomplishment.

★ Famous People Born in Oklahoma ★

Johnny Bench the baseball player, born in Oklahoma City in 1947.

Garth Brooks the singer, born in Tulsa in 1962.

Gordon Cooper the astronaut, born in Shawnee in 1927.

James Garner the actor, born in Norman in 1928.

Vince Gill the singer, born in Norman in 1957.

Ron Howard the actor and director, born in Duncan in 1954.

Jennifer Jones the actress, born in Tulsa in 1919.

Jeane Kirkpatrick the diplomat, born in Duncan in 1926.

Reba McEntire the singer, born in McAlester in 1955.

Brad Pitt the actor born in Shawnee in 1963.

Will Rogers the humorist, born in Oologah in 1879.

Maria Tallchief the ballerina, born in Fairfax in 1925.

★ Where Will You Visit? ★

★ What Photos Will You Take? ★

State Capital: Salem

State Flower: Oregon Grape

Population: 3,831,074 (Ranks 27th, as of 2010 Census)

Land Area: 95,988 square miles (Ranks 10th)

Population Density: 39.9 persons per square mile (Ranks 39th)

★ Arlie's Insight & Highlights ★

My memories of Oregon, the Beaver state, started when I was serving in the Military. I had traveled from Fort Hood, Texas to Fort Lewis, Washington by bus to prepare for an overseas assignment in Asia. We stopped at Mount Hood Ski Lodge, for a late meal. When we entered, the fireplace was burning and the atmosphere was so inviting, I thought what a fantastic way to end this day. Since then, I have had several Oregon experiences and all of them have been pleasant.

One memorable experience began when my wife and I were staying in Portland for a city tour and we had some idle time, so we walked down to the dock where a Russian Ship was at port. We had been on a long visit to the Soviet Union the previous fall, so we decided to approach some of the crew for a visit but only one of them spoke broken English. We were finally invited on the ship, with some other curious visitors and we got a full tour of this old ship. Our tour of Portland was most impressive and it is obvious how this city got a nickname, "City of Roses", I still have many great photos of the lush rose gardens there. I also remember having dinner at one of Portland's restaurants one evening and looking to the east we could see Mount Hood, it was the view of a dream world!

Most of Oregon's population is found in the fertile valley of the Willamette River, this is where Portland is located, near it's junction with the Columbia River.

A rewind to the early history of Oregon tells us that it had many problems found in other western states. The area was occupied by Native Americans (Indians) some of them have been there for hundreds, if not thousands of years. The chinook lived along the Columbia River where fishing was good. The Bannock, Cayuse, Paiute, Nez Perce and others lived east of the Cascade Mountains, while the Klamath and Modoc tribes lived near what is the southern border of present day Oregon. The Indian Wars were significant in Oregon and slowed permanent settlement in much of the state. As early as 1847, the Indians killed Marcus Whitman and 13 others near what is Walla Walla, Washington today. These killings led to the Cayuse War of 1847, where the Indian Villages were destroyed. In the 1850's, the Indians were angered by being forced from their land. Much later, in 1872-73, the Modoc War lasted eight months when white settlers tried to force the Modoc's to go on the

Klamath reservation. They resisted until the army forced them to surrender.

Some of the final resistance was the Nez Perce War of 1877, when Chief Joseph, a Nez Perce leader refused to let the Government move his people to the reservation in Idaho. He fought a running battle through Idaho and Montana, but was finally captured near the Canadian border, in Montana. The Paiute and Bannock revolted against settlers in 1878, but were soon defeated.

Some of the earliest exploration of what is present-day Oregon began as early as 1579, when Sir Francis Drake sailed the Pacific Coast of Oregon. In 1792, Robert Gray actually sailed into the Columbia River, but the greatest of the early explorers of the area was the Lewis and Clark over land trip to the Pacific Ocean in 1805. In 1811, an American fur trader, John Jacob Astor, established a fur trading post at Astoria, near the coast in northwest Oregon. Another company, the Hudson's Bay Company, a well-known British trading company, established Fort Vancouver, the present location of Vancouver, Washington. In 1825, John McLoughlin, managed this company for 20 years and he later became a U.S. citizen and he finally became known as the "Father of Oregon".

Methodist Missionaries started the first permanent American settlement in the Willamette Valley in 1834 and the first large migration came to Oregon the same year. It was estimated that about one thousand settlers came that year to settle in the fertile Willamette Valley. In the years that followed, hundreds of settlers traveled over the "Oregon Trail" to settle in this valley.

In 1846, a treaty made the 49th parallel the main boundary between British and American Territory in the Oregon Region and two years later, in 1848, Oregon became a territory. In February of 1859, Oregon became the 33rd state in the union.

The "Donation Land Law", of 1850, created great incentive to settle parts of Oregon. This law provided that any male American citizen over 18 years of age, who settled in Oregon before December, 1850, could get 320 acres of land, his wife could receive 320 acres also. To qualify for ownership he had to cultivate this land for four years, but from December 1850, to December 1855, a settler had to be 21 years old to receive land and he would only get 160 acres.

After the Civil War ended (1861-1865) soldiers from both sides found new opportunity in the west. Oregon had in 1860, about 52,000 persons, but by 1890, the state had over 300,000 residents,

Oregon has various types of land regions (geography). The Columbia Plateau, covers about half of eastern Oregon, most is high and dry wheat country. The basin and range area covers parts of southeastern Oregon that is semi-arid.

The Cascade Range Mountains runs from Washington to California north to south across Oregon and are rugged volcanic peaks, the highest is Mount Hood (11,235 ft.). The coast range runs next to the Pacific Ocean, it is an area of great timber; Fir, Spruce, hemlock and other evergreen trees. The Willamette lowlands are gently rolling farm and forest areas where more than half of the state's population live, it has rich soil and a great climate that make it the most important farming and industrial area in the state.

For the visitor to Oregon, there is so much to see in its natural beauty, I will always remember our visit to Crater Lake. We arrived early in the morning and the fog shrouded the lake, creating a mystical scene. I struggled to find Wizard Island, but had to wait for more than an hour and finally it appeared!

Some major points of interest are; Fort Clatsop National Memorial, near Astoria, McLoughlin House National Historic site near Oregon City, all of the Mount Hood area, the John Day Fossil Beds National Monument (three separate locations), the High Desert Museum, near Bend and don't miss "Crater Lake National Park" the crown of the cascades. On the west coast of Oregon, are the Sea Lion Caves and the Oregon Dunes National Recreation area.

If the visitor likes ocean scenery, highway 101 is the ultimate drive all the way into California. Oregon is truly a pacific jewel.

★ Kelly's Perspective & Lessons Learned ★

I am looking forward to a return trip to Oregon. We have good friends that have moved to the state and really enjoy the end-to-end beauty.

★ Famous People Born in Oregon ★

Matt Groening the cartoonist, born in Portland in 1954.

Joni Huntley the track athlete, born in McMinnville in 1956.

David Kennerly the photographer, born in Roseburg in 1947.

Dave Kingman the baseball player, born in Pendleton in 1948.

Phyllis McGinley the author, born in Ontario in 1905.

Linus Carl Pauling the chemist, born in Portland in 1901.

Jane Powell the actressand singer, born in Portland in 1929.

Steve Prefontaine the track athlete, born in Coos Bay in 1951.

Doc Severinsen the band leader, born in Arlington in 1927.

Sally Stanford the politician, born in Baker City in 1903.

Sally Struthers the actress, born in Portland in 1947.

★ Where Will You Visit? ★

★ What Photos Will You Take? ★

State Capital: Harrisburg

State Flower: Mountain Laurel

Population: 12,702,379 (Ranks 6th, as of 2010 Census)

Land Area: 44,742.7 square miles (Ranks 32nd)

Population Density: 283.9 persons per square mile (Ranks 9th)

★ Arlie's Insight & Highlights ★

Pennsylvania, the Keystone State, was named because it was the center of the arch formed by the original 13 American States. It is one of the greatest historical centers of our country. So many things happened first in Pennsylvania, it could be called the state of "First". A few examples that stand out include: the first and second Continental Congress meeting in the city of

Philadelphia before and during the War for Independence from Great Britain in addition to the fact that Philadelphia is the true birthplace of the United States of America and served as the capital from 1790 to 1800, when the capital moved to Washington, D.C.

A view in the very early history of Pennsylvania and the surrounding region, one can see several western European countries were interested in this area. Among them were: the British, French, Swedish, Spanish and Netherlands. In 1643, the Swedish settlers established a capital in a small area known as "Tinicum" Island at what is now Philadelphia. This was the capital of their colony of New Sweden. In 1665, the Dutch troops came from New Netherlands and captured New Sweden. The Dutch held this Pennsylvania area until 1664, when the English captured it for the British. The English Duke of York controlled this Pennsylvania region until 1681, during that year (1681) King Charles II of England granted this region to William Penn in payment of a debt to Penn's father. Penn called this area "Sylvania" (means woods). King Charles added Penn to the name in honor of Penn's father, an English Admiral.

William Penn, was a "Quaker", who wanted his people to have freedom of worship in this new land. He also wanted religious freedom for persons of other faiths and the people of Pennsylvania to have personal rights, property rights and self-government. It appears Penn had special foresight in dealing with the Native Americans (Indians) in that he arranged a Treaty of Friendship with them in an area known as lower Kensington.

William Penn made several trips out of the new country back to England. On Penn's return to Pennsylvania in 1699, he later wrote a new constitution, called the "Charter of Privileges" (1701), this constitution had many changes, including greater control of the government by the people. William Penn went back to England again in 1701, and died there in 1718. Penn's family governed Pennsylvania until the Revolutionary War began in 1775.

In the 1700's English Colonist fought many wars against the French and France's Indian allies. The French and Indian War began in western Pennsylvania in 1754. In 1755, the French and Indians ambushed and killed most of General Braddock's Soldiers on the Monongahela River. Fighting continued in the colony until 1758, when the French withdrew from the colony. The war ended in 1763, with a British Victory. Pennsylvania brought land from the Indians in the Fort Stanwix Treaty of 1768 and this treaty settled most of the Indian troubles in the colony.

In the mid 1700's, the British imposed new taxes and trade restrictions on the American Colonies and the Colonies united to oppose these new taxes. Leaders from the Colonies met to discuss how they would resist these new British laws. With the meeting of the "First Continental Congress", on September 5, 1774, they voted to stop all trade with Great Britain.

The Revolutionary War began in April, 1775. In May 1775, the second Continental Congress met in Philadelphia and the delegates voted for independence from Great Britain, on July 4, 1776. Many turbulent years follow the Declaration of Independence with much blood-shed and suffering.

British Troops captured Philadelphia in September, 1777, and held the city until June of 1778. General Washington and his troops suffered through a bitter winter of 1777-78 at Valley Forge during the Revolutionary War. The tide of the war finally turned after many battles in favor of the Colonists and help from France. The war ended for the U.S. in April 1783, with victory at York Town.

After the Revolutionary War was over, the Constitution Convention met in Philadelphia from May to September of 1787, to write and approve the United States Constitution. Pennsylvania was the second state to approve the U.S. Constitution on December 12, 1787. Following the end of the Revolutionary War, Pennsylvania was a center of the Nations growth. In 1859, the nation's first commercially successful oil well was completed, near Titusville.

During the Civil War (1861-65) Pennsylvania, firmly opposed slavery and was among the leaders of the "Abolitionist Movement". Only New York sent more troops to the Union Army than the state of Pennsylvania. In June 1863, General Lee led a powerful Confederate Army into southern Pennsylvania and on July 1, Union Forces under General Meade met the Confederates at Gettysburg, and in the three-day battle that followed, was one of the bloodiest in history, it broke the strength of the Confederacy.

After the Civil War, Pennsylvania prospered; it became a leading producer of oil, aluminum and steel. Thousands of immigrants came into the state, cities and towns grew rapidly. The state has two major industrial areas, one on the east side (Philadelphia) and one on the west side (Pittsburgh). These two metro areas produce more than some entire states; they would be described as amazing.

The geography of Pennsylvania is generally hilly, but in geographic terms, about half of the state, western and northern part, is Appalachian Plateau, the central and eastern is mainly Appalachian ridge and valley region and the southern part is Piedmont. Some small and special areas are; Atlantic Costal Plains in extreme southeast part and the Erie lowlands runs along Lake Erie into New York, this is a great area for fruits and vegetables.

For the traveler (visitor) to Pennsylvania, there is so much to see and do. The distance across the state is more than 300 miles. The visitor should get a good state map and some good city maps of the cities one intends to visit; it's a must for Pittsburgh and Philadelphia. In Pittsburgh parking is a great challenge, even on guided tours; our bus was required to park for short periods on the main roads. Many of the roads in Pittsburgh run parallel to the river and two major rivers merge at the down-town area, it can be a great challenge to the new visitor. The city of Pittsburgh could be a one stop vacation spot all in one great area. There is much about art and music, with 5 downtown theaters and several museums and art centers.

If you like photography and can do only one exciting thing while in town, take one of the "inclines" to the top of Mount Washington and get the view of the beautiful skyline. Either of the two most famous inclines rises about 400 ft. over the city and river area from Station Square.

One of the most interesting visits to any college or university was the visit to the University of Pittsburgh. Here is where the special class rooms were decorated in relation to the country it represented, such as: Germany, France, Italy, Egypt, et al., we were duly impressed.

We have been in the Philadelphia area two times, but regrettably, we have not toured the city, this call for a revisit! We don't count it until we have toured the city.

Other places the visitor may wish to travel; The George Washington Grist Mill at Perryopolis, Fort Necessity National Battlefield at Farmington, Drake Well Memorial Park. at Titusville, Fort Roberdeau, near Tyrone and Gettysburg National Military Park, at Gettysburg.

Other places of interest: The Cornwall Furnace at Cornwall, Indian Echo Caverns, near Middletown, Onyx Cave and Crystal Cave, near Kutztown, Washington Crossing State Historic site, near Newtown, Valley Forge National Historic Park, near Forge and all of Philadelphia, where we must return some day to visit the "Cradle of America", lets enjoy the journey.

★ Famous People Born in Pennsylvania ★

Louisa May Alcott the author, born in Germantown in 1832.

John Barrymore the actor, born in Philadelphia in 1882.

James Buchanan the 15th U.S. president, born in Mercersburg in 1791.

Mary Cassatt the painter, born in Allegheny in 1844.

Bill Cosby the actor, born in Philadelphia in 1937.

Gene Kelly the dancer and actor, born in Pittsburgh in 1912.

Jim Kelly the football player, born in East Brady in 1960.

Arnold Palmer the golfer, born in Youngstown 1929.

Betsy Griscom Ross the flagmaker, born in Philadelphia in 1752.

Gertrude Stein the author, born in Allegheny in 1874.

John Updike the author, born in Shillington in 1932.

★ Where Will You Visit? ★

_____
_____
_____
_____

★ What Photos Will You Take? ★

_____
_____
_____
_____

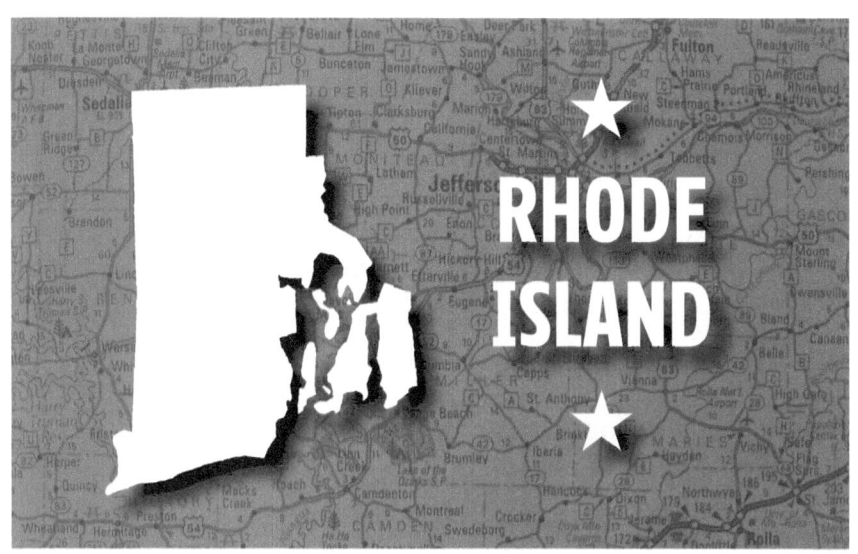

State Capital: Providence

State Flower: Violet

Population: 1,052,567 (Ranks 43rd, as of 2010 Census)

Land Area: 1033.8 square miles (Ranks 50th)

Population Density: 1018.1 persons per square mile (Ranks 2nd)

★ Arlie's Insight & Highlights ★

Rhode Island is the smallest of our states, and makes up for its size in many ways. The early history of this state tells the story of the key position it played in the founding of our country. Roger Williams, who founded Providence in 1636, worked for political and religious freedoms. In 1776, Rhode Island became the first of the 13 original colonies to declare independence from the mother country, Great Britain. Rhode Island did not ratify the constitution until 1790, when the Bill of Rights was added to the U.S. Constitution.

Roger Williams and his companions founded the first Baptist church in America, "Soul Liberty", which was and continues to be, its watchword. We had the privilege of attending services in the present building, completed in May 1775, where the Charitable Baptist Society secured its charter from the colonial legislature, allowing it to own property.

One of the early industries to be established was textiles by Sam Slater, when in the late 1700s he built the first cotton spinning mill driven by water power. Rhode Islanders were instrumental in shipping, whaling, and boat building. The Dodge Brothers started the American jewelry industry in Providence, Rhode Island.

Newport, Rhode Island is also a fascinating place to visit. History tells us, that Newport was 10 degrees cooler in summer than

the surrounding area and 10 degrees warmer in the winter than the surrounding area. I can see where this temperature difference would be important, before all the modern creature comforts, such as air conditioning, were invented. After two visits to this state, we decided we would spend several days in Newport, in order to see all the Newport Mansions that were open for a fee. Most of these mansions are along Bellevue Avenue. Hunter House, located on the north end of town at 54 Washington Street, is a national historic landmark. It was built in 1748, by the Deputy Governor of Rhode Island. Near the north end of Bellevue Avenue, is Kingscote, a Gothic Revival cottage built in 1839, acquired by William King in 1864. This is a national historic landmark and it contains many original family furnishings.

As one continues south on Bellevue Avenue on the west side is "The Elms"; this is also a national historic landmark, built in 1901 as a summer residence for Edward Berwin, who made his fortune in Pennsylvania Coal. The grounds feature special trees and a collection of statuary. "The Elms" is often beautifully decorated for Christmas. Chateau-sur-mer, is supposed to be one of the finest examples of Victorian Architecture in America. It was built in 1852 for William Wetmore, who made his fortune in China Trade. This estate went through extensive renovation by Richard Hunt in 1872.

Also on Bellevue Avenue is the beautiful "Rosecliff". Rosecliff was built in 1902 for Mrs. Hermann Oelrichs. It was designed by Stanford White after the "Grand Trianon" at Versailles, France. This glazed terracotta mansion was a gift by Mr. and Mrs. J. Edgar Monroe of New Orleans.

"Marble House", one of the most gracious of Newport's cottages, was completed in 1892 for Mr. and Mrs. William K. Vanderbilt. This property was designed by Richard Morris Hunt and it still contains much of its original furnishings and Harold Vanderbilt's yachting memorabilia.

The Chinese Teahouse on the cliffs overlooking the Atlantic Ocean was built in 1913. This teahouse is where we had a quick lunch break on our visit to Marble House. We just pretended that we were having a picnic in our back yard; what a dream it was, as we looked out over the ocean.

"The Breakers" is a national historic landmark that was built in 1895 for Mr. and Mrs. Cornelius Vanderbilt II. It was designed by Richard Hunt and was modeled after 16th century Northern Italian palaces. This estate overlooks the Atlantic Ocean and the famous Cliff Walk. The Breakers stable and carriage house was built in 1895, by Mr. Hunt, the same man that designed the Breakers. This building, fully equipped and staffed, was an important addition to the Breakers. It holds the private collection of Vanderbilt memorabilia, including their famous coach, "Venture". On rare occasions, the Preservation Society of Newport County will open a new historic house. Two such houses were opened to the public in 1998. Please keep in mind most of these homes have variable schedules. The two new ones are Chepstow and the Isaac Bell House.

The Chepstow is an Italian-style villa and was designed by George Mason. Chepstow was built in 1860. In 1911 the house was acquired by Mrs. Emily Morris Gallatin and it was donated to the Society in 1986 by Alletta Morris McBean.

The Isaac Bell House is one of the finest examples of the Shingle Style architecture in America. It is a national historic landmark and was completed in 1883 for Isaac Bell.

Also in Newport is the Green Animal Topiary Garden. This topiary garden was started by Thomas Brayton about 1880. There are 80 sculptured trees and shrubs, including 21 animal shapes that give the historic country estate its name. Highlights include the formal flower beds, fruit and vegetable garden, and a small gift shop.

The Hammersmith Farm, on Harrison Ave., is far removed from the other Newport mansions, but it is a mansion of Victorian style. It was the childhood home of Jacqueline Bouvier Kennedy Onassis. Although this property hosted the wedding reception of Jacqueline and John F. Kennedy, they were married in town at St. Mary's Roman Catholic Parish. Further, and during his presidency, Kennedy spent enough time at Hammersmith Farm that it was referred to as the "Summer White House".

The "Astors' Beechwood" was built in 1851 for New York merchant Daniel Parris. It later became the summer estate of the Astor family. Beechwood became the showplace for many of

Mrs. Astor's dinner parties after many renovations by Richard Morris Hunt. When Mrs. Astor died, she left the mansion to her son John Jacob Astor IV, who married his second wife Madeline in its ballroom. After John's death on the Titanic in 1912, it passed to his widow Madeline, who turned the entire third floor into her own personal walk-in closet. During the summer months while the Astor family is living in the Mansion, Astor family members give tours to guests. Further, everyone living and working in the mansion, acts as though it is 1891 and acts out the character throughout the tour. Belcourt Castle is a property designed by Richard Morris Hunt and is located at 657 Bellevue Avenue. The structure began in 1891 and was completed in 1894. The original cost was $3.2 million in 1894, equivalent to $80 million in 2011. Belcourt was built for thirty-three year old Oliver Belmont, who was still a bachelor, at the completion of this 50,000 square foot, 60 room summer villa. It was designed in a multitude of European styles and periods. This mixture of design is said to be of French, German, English, and Italian influence. Belmont married Alva Vanderbilt, the former wife of William Vanderbilt, in January 1896. Alva made many changes to Belcourt, creating a hybrid mixture of styles. Mrs. Belmont died in France in 1933 and the mansion passed to 80 year old Perry Belmont, who removed most of the contents and auctioned off more. In 1940 Belcourt began to change owners. In November 1956, the Lorillards sold Belcourt Castle to the Tinney family. In May 2009, Mr. Tinney put Belcourt up for sale again and it was purchased by Carolyn Rafaelian who is restoring and renovating the mansion and reopened it in the summer of 2014.

Our visit to Belcourt Castle occurred while the Tinneys owned it. We arrived too early for admission so we waited in the rose garden, where workers were busy tending the roses, when a man came hobbling up and said he sprained his foot. This man turned out to be Mr. Tinney. We had a nice long visit in the morning shade, before our tour began.

As we departed Newport that day, I thought we have never seen this much elegant history in one place.

★ Kelly's Perspective & Lessons Learned ★

Building on what my Dad has written about the remarkable mansions in Newport, I have to share a few notes and a photo of my favorite property which is Rosecliff. Noteworthy, the mansion was completed over 4 years - in 1902, with the central portion of the home dedicated to Newport's largest ballroom at 40 by 80 feet, which is still used today for special occasions. As an example, the 1974 version of *The Great Gatsby* showcased the

ballroom as well as a portion of the amazing Rosecliff grounds that border the ocean.

If you appreciate grand architecture, you will be fascinated by the Preservation Society of Newport County's investment and results. They are a non-profit organization that lives up to their mission:

> Great Houses connect people to a nation's heritage and open windows to another age.

The Preservation Society of Newport County is a non-profit organization whose mission is to protect, preserve, and present an exceptional collection of house museums and landscapes in one of the most historically intact cities in America.

★ Famous People Born in Rhode Island ★

Harry Anderson the actor, born in Newport in 1952.

George M. Cohan the actor and dramatist, born in Providence in 1878.

Robert Gray the sea captain, born in Tiverton in 1755.

Spalding Gray the writer and performance artist, born in Barrington in 1941.

Bobby Hackett the trumpeter, born in Providence in 1915.

Van Johnson the actor, born in Newport in 1916.

Irving R. Levine the news correspondent, born in Pawtucket in 1922.

H. P. Lovecraft the author, born in Providence in 1890.

Ida Lewis the lighthouse keeper, born in Newport in 1842.

Dana C. Munro the educator and historian, born in Bristol in 1866.

Matthew C. Perry the naval officer, born in Newport in 1794.

Oliver Hazard Perry the naval officer, born in South Kingstown 1785.

★ Where Will You Visit? ★

★ What Photos Will You Take? ★

State Capital: Columbia

State Flower: Carolina Jessamine

Population: 4,625,364 (Ranks 40th, as of 2010 Census)

Land Area: 30,060.7 square miles (Ranks 40th)

Population Density: 153.9 persons per square mile (Ranks 20th)

★ Arlie's Insight & Highlights ★

South Carolina, the Palmetto State, has a turbulent history in the past two major wars fought on American soil; the Revolutionary War and the American Civil War. Several major battles were fought here during the Revolutionary War, Colonial Victories in the battle of "Kings Mountain" and the battle of "Cowpens" were the turning points of the war in the southern region of the Colonies. Some historians say the nickname "Palmetto State", came as a result of events occurring about

1776, when a small fort constructed of palmetto logs defeated the British Fleet that attempted to capture Charleston Harbor. The day after the battle the colonial commander saw a column of smoke from the burning British Ship, which reminded him of the Palmetto tree.

At the beginning of the Civil War, South Carolina was the first state to secede from the union, actually before the war on December 20, 1860 and the Confederate Troops fired the first shot on Fort Sumter in Charleston Harbor on April 12, 1861. By the spring of 1861, ten other southern states had joined the secession movement and joined to form the Confederate States of America. After the war started, fighting raged along the coast in South Carolina throughout the war. Late in the war (1865) General William Sherman destroyed many of the homes and plantations in South Carolina and burned Columbia, the State Capital. It was estimated that about 25% of South Carolina total troops died in this war.

South Carolina, was one of the early admissions to the union, but seceded during the conflict in late 1860, and was readmitted to the union on June 25, 1868. This was very similar to the other states that seceded during the civil war. Growth was slow to recover in South Carolina, but businessmen began expanding the textile industry and electrical power became the source of energy for many textile mills. Cheap labor in the south caused several textile companies to move from northern states to South Carolina.

The geography of South Carolina is reasonably simple. The eastern two-thirds of the state is low lands, called "Atlantic Costal Plains", swamps cover much of the land near the coast and extend inland along the many rivers. The Piedmont covers most of northwestern South Carolina. The Piedmont slopes from northwest to southeast and the "Fall Line" is found on the eastern edge of the Piedmont. This fall line is an area where rivers come off of the higher region to the lower lands, and the rivers flow more rapidly. The third, smaller region of the state is "The Blue Ridge Area", which includes the mountains that run from Georgia to Pennsylvania.

Tobacco is the state's main crop; however soybeans, cotton, corn and peaches are important to the South Carolina. Traveling around Greenville and Spartanburg is definitely fruit country.

South Carolina's, gardens are some of the most beautiful attractions and here are a few of the most famous: Cypress Gardens, Magnolia Gardens, and Middleton Gardens. The Middleton Place Gardens are said to be the oldest landscape gardens in the U.S. starting in 1741, they feature azaleas, camellias and some ancient oak trees. The Brookgreen Gardens, near Georgetown, covers part of three rice plantations. The

Edisto Gardens are in Orangeburg and display camellias roses, azaleas, and many other flowers.

Other primary attractions for the visitor would be old forts; Fort Sumter in Charleston Harbor, Fort Moultrie, same location and Fort Johnston, is the place where colonists seized tax stamps from the British in 1765 opposing the stamp act.

If we are able to return to this area, we would visit the coastline from Charleston, then north to Myrtle Beach on the northern coast of South Carolina.

For the visitor (traveler), a trip to South Carolina is a place where one can enjoy the rich, early history of our country from Revolutionary time through the Civil War times and into the gracious, experience of the present. Take this journey!

★ Famous People Born in South Carolina ★

Whisperin' Bill Anderson the songwriter, born in Columbia in 1937.

Bernard Baruch the statesman, born in Camden 1870.

James "Godfather" Brown the singer, born in Barnwell in 1933.

Joseph H. Burckhalter the inventor, born in Columbia in 1912.

Joe Frazier the prize fighter, born in Beaufort in 1944.

Althea Gibson the tennis champion, born in Silver in 1927.

Dizzy Gillespie the jazz trumpeter, born in Cheraw in 1917.

Charlayne Hunter-Gault the journalist, born in Due West in 1942.

Andrew Jackson 7th U.S. president, born in Waxhaw in 1767.

Francis "Swamp Fox" Marion the general, born in Berkeley County in 1732.

Ronald McNair the astronaut, born in Lake City in 1950.

Strom Thurmond the politician, born in Edgefield in 1902.

★ Where Will You Visit? ★

_____
_____
_____
_____

★ What Photos Will You Take? ★

_____
_____
_____
_____

State Capital: Pierre

State Flower: American Pasque Flower

Population: 814,180 (Ranks 46th, as of 2010 Census)

Land Area: 75,811 square miles (Ranks 16th)

Population Density: 10.7 persons per square mile (Ranks 46th)

★ Arlie's Insight & Highlights ★

South Dakota, the Sunshine State, has great diversity, although it is part of the mid-western states, it is much like what one thinks of as the "Old West". If one remembers the past history of South Dakota, the colorful characters include: Wild Bill Hickok, Sitting Bull, George Custer and Calamity Jane, just to name a few. The cities around the Black Hills even ring of history from by-gone-days; Custer, Rapid City,

Lead and Deadwood all have a colorful history.

All of the past exciting history of the Black Hills, only adds to the reason this area is such a great vacation journey. In our travels we have enjoyed every day of this unique place. I emphasize unique because the state has lots of sites you cannot find in any of the other 50 states. Some of the attractions are; Mount Rushmore National Memorial, where one finds the head carvings of George Washington, Thomas Jefferson, Theodore Roosevelt and Abraham Lincoln. A short distance away, near Custer, is a larger statue of the Sioux Chief, "Crazy Horse", being carved out of a granite mountain. Also, nearby are the exciting caves; Jewel Cave National Monument, Wind Cave National Park and Rushmore Cave. Southeast of Rapid city the visitor will find the "Badlands National Park" and the site of the Wounded Knee Massacre, near Batesland. One of the best passion plays we have seen in our travels is found at Spearfish, it's called The Black Hills Passion Play.

Other interesting areas in the state for visitors would be in north central, South Dakota, near Mobridge, where one finds Sitting Bull's grave and the Sacajawea Monument, also the "Verendrye Monument", near the capital, Pierre. In the fertile area of eastern South Dakota, are other places of interest for the visitor, they include; little town on the prairie, near De Smet, Noble's Trail Monument, near Woonsocket and the "Corn Palace" at Mitchell.

The geography of South Dakota, is composed of four major land forms; the " Great Plains' covers about 65-70% of the state's western part, with the exception of a small area of isolated mountains, known as the "Black Hills" area in west central South Dakota. The "Young Drift Plains" runs north to south along the eastern side of the state parallel to the James River, and the "Dissected Till Plains" covers the southeastern corner

of the state. This area is where the glaciers left large deposits of till (soil) and wind-blown soil over the area, and over time streams have dissected (cut-up) the region. Some of this area is very fertile and makes good crop lands. Farmers in this area of South Dakota harvest the most corn, oats and soybeans. The majority of South Dakota's crops are grown east of the Missouri River, however, federal irrigation projects have made the land in some of the state's western areas favorable for growing crops like corn, alfalfa, barley and oats.

It is easier to understand the settlement of South Dakota when we look back at some of the state's early history. As early as

1682, a French explorer, Robert Caveller, claimed for France all the land drained by the Mississippi River and the land included the region of South Dakota. In 1743, two brothers, Francois and Louis La Verendrye were the first white men to actually visit this South Dakota region. In 1803, the United States acquired South Dakota and much more from France in the famous "Louisiana Purchase". In 1804, President Thomas Jefferson sent Lewis and Clark to explore the Louisiana Territory and find a trail to the Pacific Ocean.

The first settlement in South Dakota was founded in 1817 by a French fur trader, Joseph La Framboise, it was located at the junction of the Bad River and the Missouri River, at the present site of Pierre. Congress created the Dakota Territory in 1861, and by 1868, the Laramie Treaty ended the Red Cloud War. A few years later (1874) gold was discovered in the Black Hills, thousands of people came seeking gold, but others came to settle the land. From 1878 and later many came for public lands offered by the government. In 1870 the region had about 12,000 residents, and by 1890 it had more than 340,000 people. Many settlers came from neighboring states, but many were immigrants from Norway, Russia, Germany, Britain and other western European countries. South Dakota became the 40th state in the union on November 2, 1889.

Plan to visit this friendly state and enjoy the memorable geographic and historic sites.

★ Famous People Born in South Dakota ★

Sparky Anderson the baseball manager, born in Bridgewater 1934.

Tom Brokaw the TV newscaster, born in Webster in 1940.

Joe Foss the governor and 1st Commissioner of the American Football League, born in Sioux Falls in 1915.

Crazy Horse the Oglala chief, born about 1840.

Oscar Howe the Sioux artist, born in Joe Creek in 1915.

Hubert H. Humphrey the senator and vice president, born in Wallace in 1911.

Cheryl Ladd the actress, born in Huron in 1951.

Ward L. Lambert the basketball and baseball coach, born in Deadwood in 1888.

George McGovern the politician, born in Avon in 1922.

Rain-in-the-Face the Hunkpapa Sioux chief, born along the Cheyenne River about 1835.

Red Cloud the Oglala Sioux chief, born near North Platte in 1822.

Sitting Bull the Hunkpappa Sioux chief, born near the Grand River about 1831.

Mamie Van Doren the actress, born in Rowena in 1931.

★ Where Will You Visit? ★

_____
_____
_____
_____

★ What Photos Will You Take? ★

_____
_____
_____
_____

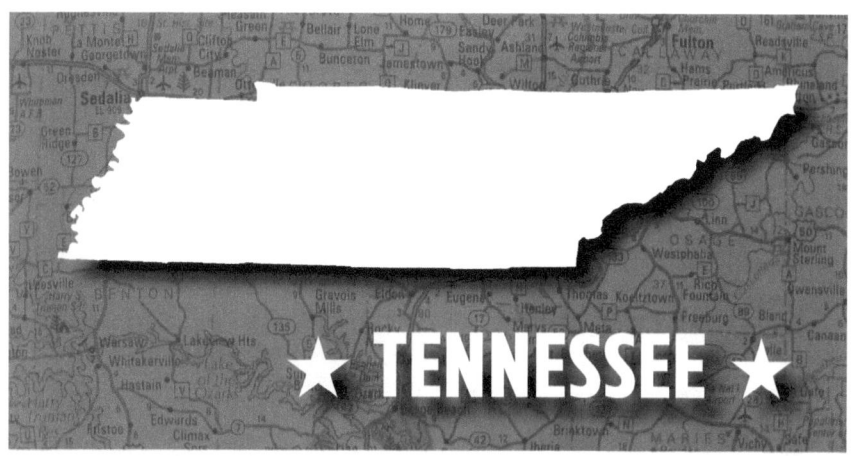

State Capital: Nashville

State Flower: Iris

Population: 6,346,105 (Ranks 17th, as of 2010 Census)

Land Area: 41,234.9 square miles (Ranks 34th)

Population Density: 153.9 persons per square mile (Ranks 19th)

★ Arlie's Insight & Highlights ★

Tennessee, is truly the volunteer State. The nickname is well deserved when we look back at the history of the state and the brave and courageous men who served Tennessee and beyond its boundaries. Names that will be indelible in the history of America. Some of the luminaries to grace the history books are John Sevier of the Revolutionary War Era, Andrew Jackson in the war of 1812, and Sargent Alvin York, of World War I fame. The Texas Revolution benefited from two great heroes, Davy Crockett and Sam Houston who grew up in Tennessee

and died in the line-of-duty for their country. Tennessee is aptly called the volunteer state because of its great and colorful military traditions.

A very early history of the Tennessee Region, like much of the present mid-west, was occupied by Indians now known as the "Mound Builders". The Mound Builders use mounds to support their temples and some houses. It is claimed that when the first white explorers came to the region they saw some of the early Chickasaw and Cherokee people still building mounds. As early as 1540, Spanish explorers (De-Soto) were traveling through Tennessee to the west and did reach the Mississippi River in 1541, although they soon left the area. Many years later (1673), two English explorers arrived to evaluate the Tennessee River and Valley area.

In 1673, when the English were exploring the Tennessee River Valley, the French, Louis Joliet and Father Marquette, were coming down the Mississippi River from the north. In 1682 Robert Cavelier De La Salle claimed the entire Mississippi Valley for France. French settlers began moving into the Mississippi Valley, a place they called "New France". In 1714, the French set up a trading post close to what is now Nashville. This region became a three-way contest, with France, Spain and Britain claiming the Tennessee Region. The dispute finally turned out to be between France and Britain. The result, was the French and Indian War broke out between British and French settlers in 1754. The British out-numbered the French and after nine long-bloody years the British won and in 1763 with the "Treaty of Paris", the French gave Britain all claim to the lands east of the Mississippi River.

During the War of 1812 with the British, Andrew Jackson led the U.S. Forces to defeat the British Army at the battle of New Orleans. The Tennesseans supported Jackson when he ran for President and won in 1828. Andrew Jackson fought for the rights of the poor and was active in helping the state and the Nation grow.

In the Civil War Days, the people of Tennessee were divided in their sympathy between the north and the south, however, the war spread across the state's middle and western regions.

As the war spread, fierce battles would occur on Tennessee soil. In 1862, the battle of Shiloh was one of those. The Confederates lost more than 10,000 men, including a General (Albert Johnston) and the union lost more than 13,000 soldiers. After this union victory, federal control of west Tennessee was assured and President Lincoln appointed Andrew Johnson the Military Governor of Tennessee. In 1863, General Grant won Battles at Lookout Mountain and captured Chattanooga after three days of fighting. In 1864, General Sherman's troops went from Chattanooga into Georgia and captured Atlanta.

On April 14, 1865, President Lincoln was assassinated and Andrew Johnson was inaugurated as President on April 15, of 1865. Then President Johnson declared the rebellion in Tennessee at an end on June 13, 1865. Many of the state's plantations in western Tennessee were divided into smaller farms. The farmers had to plant their own cotton and other crops. Although some farmers had depended on slaves, progress was slow on farms and it took nearly 40 years for Tennessee's farms to recover from the war period. A note to remember about Tennessee is that it was the last state to secede from the union (June 8, 1861), but the state was the first to be readmitted to the union on July 24, 1866. Tennessee was a member of the union very early, from June 1, 1796, until it seceded in June of 1861.

Unknown too many in our country is the fact that part of eastern Tennessee was a separate state at one time in the past. John Sevier, was Tennessee's first governor and served six terms. He was also the first governor of the State of "Franklin", now a part of Tennessee. Franklin broke away from North Carolina in 1784 and it was an independent state until 1788.

Traveling in Tennessee is easy, we have visited the state many times over the years and we have found something new to enjoy on each trip. I will cover some of the primary attractions we have discovered in different regions of the state; on the west side of the state is the great city of Memphis that overlooks the mighty Mississippi. Our special visit here was downtown and to Graceland, home of Elvis Presley. Here we had the great tour of the Mansion and grounds. We also had photos taken in Elvis's Pink Jeep, we were able to visit the aircraft "Lisa Marie" and it was the total Presley experience. In Jackson, Tennessee,

the high-light was "Casey Jones Home" and Rail Road Museum of the Railroad Hero of the Famous Folk Ballad and his fatal ride.

On to Nashville where one can visit the "Grand Ole Opry House" this is where we took a special flight one Christmas to enjoy what was called a "Country Christmas". We spent a week being treated like Kings and Queens, What an Experience!

On another trip to Nashville, we toured the Hermitage, the Stately Home of President Andrew Jackson. The home built in 1818 and rebuilt again in 1835. Another tour was to the "Parthenon" built in 1897 for the Tennessee Centennial; it is the world's only reproduction of the Greek Temple.

In eastern Tennessee you will find a visitor's paradise. There are so many historic sites and modern day play grounds, it's difficult to choose what to do first. Near Sevierville is the park, known as "Dollywood", you must see this one and close by is Gatlinburg another must-see area. We may be back to visit sooner than expected, as my wife saw a doll in the window at Gatlinburg, Tennessee gift shop and she has been tugging at me to go back ever since!

Also, one of the greatest national parks from our point of view is the "Great Smokey Mountain Nation Park", in eastern Tennessee and North Carolina. Tennessee is more than 450 miles west-east and there is a great diversity of terrain in this state and so much for everyone to see. Here is hoping you enjoy Tennessee as much as we have.

★ Famous People Born in Tennessee ★

Hattie Caraway the first elected woman senator, born in Bakerville in 1878.

Davy Crockett the frontiersman, born in Green City in 1786.

Sam Davis the confederate scout, born in Smyrna in 1842.

Morgan Freeman the actor, born in Memphis in 1937.

Aretha Franklin the singer, born in Memphis in 1942.

Isaac Hayes the composer, born in Covington in 1942.

Barbara Howar the broadcaster and writer, born in Nashville in 1934.

Dolly Parton the singer, born in Sevierville in 1946.

Wilma Rudolph the runner, born in St. Bethlehem in 1940.

Sequoyah the Cherokee scholar and educator, born near Knoxville about 1770.

Cybil Shepherd the actress, born in Memphis in 1950.

Tina Turner the singer, born in Brownsville in 1939.

★ Where Will You Visit? ★

★ What Photos Will You Take? ★

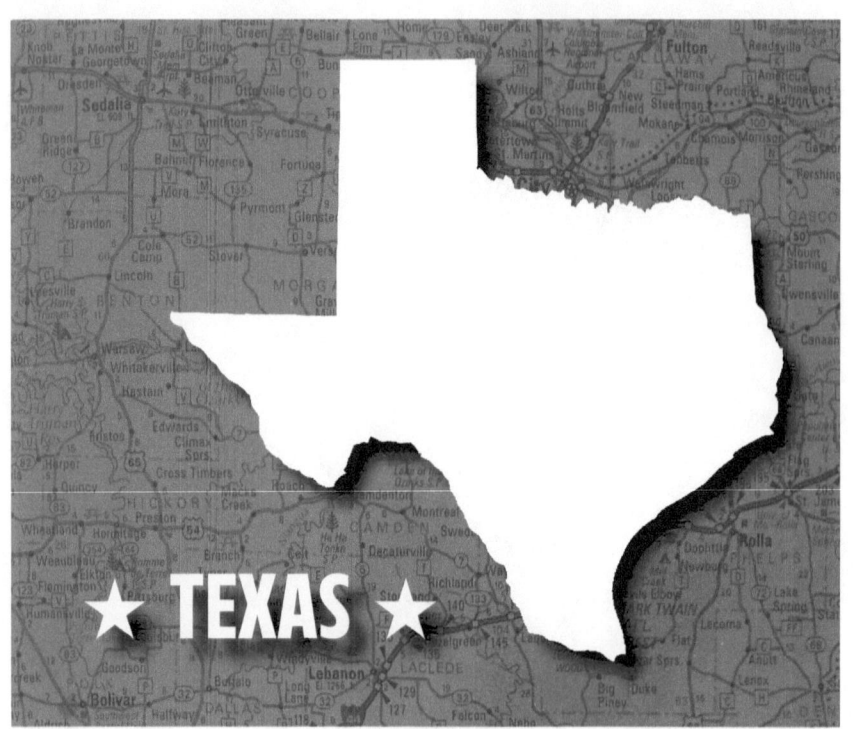

State Capital: Austin

State Flower: Bluebonnet

Population: 25,145,561 (Ranks 2nd, as of 2010 Census)

Land Area: 261,231.7 square miles (Ranks 2nd)

Population Density: 96.3 persons per square mile (Ranks 26th)

★ Arlie's Insight & Highlights ★

Texas is the second largest state in the union and one of my top 5 for diversity of landmarks, topography, and history. A few examples follow; Texas has more farms and farmed area than any other state in America. There are many surface crops but some of the major ones are cotton, cattle, sheep, fruits, and vegetables. Most of the fruits and vegetables are found in the Rio Grande Valley of South Texas. Subsurface mineral crops are very important to the entire nation. Large amounts of oil and gas are found over most of the state.

The Lone Star State has a long and turbulent history. Six flags have flown over the state in times past: Spain, France, Mexico, Texas Republic, Confederate States of America and the United States. Texas was part of Mexico when the first Americans settled there in 1836, when Jim Bowie, Davy Crockett and many others died at the Alamo to get free from Mexico. After the Alamo, Sam Houston led the Texans to defeat the Mexicans, with the battle cry of "Remember the Alamo". It's approximately 700 miles from Houston to El Paso, east to west, and 750 miles from Amarillo to Brownsville, north to south. In between all those miles there is much to see. In east Texas, from Longview to Houston, there are many beautiful pine tree forests and many lakes. From Galveston to Brownsville, there are many beautiful beaches covering hundreds of miles. Texas has several primary attractions: the Big Bend National Park is near Alpine, in the bend of the Rio Grande River. Guadalupe National Park is in far west Texas, near El Paso. Congress established the Padre Island Seashores as a National Park in 1962. It runs along the coast for about 80 miles. This area has long beaches and many sand dunes and it is like one big, beautiful sand box!

The Alamo is an Old Spanish Mission in downtown San Antonio. It is the location of a famous battle fought in 1836 during the Texas Revolution. Near Houston is the Lyndon Johnson Space Center that attracts many visitors. It is the NASA Headquarters for all the manned space projects. The visitors' center has displays of spacecraft and projects of past flights and

moon landings. Also near Houston, is the San Jacinto Monument that honors all the Texans who fought in the Battle of San Jacinto, which was the decisive battle where Texas won its independence from Mexico.

Texas has several large cities, with many places for recreation. In Arlington, one can find the well-known amusement park "Six Flags Over Texas". Houston also has some great recreation areas. San Antonio has "Sea World" attractions for travelers. Dallas has Fair Park, the home of its state fair and the Cotton Bowl, a football stadium that gets national coverage with rival football teams of Oklahoma and University of Texas each year.

One of the most fun visits we ever had was a visit to the TV set of Southfork Ranch, from the television show, *Dallas*, near Plano. This TV show was a very popular series and this visit to the location was years after the show was over. The tour began with nine participants on the tour bus, but the bus broke down and the tour company sent a beautiful stretch limousine to rescue our group. Next, when this limo pulled into the Southfork Ranch location, all the people at the concession stands and the operators all headed toward the limo, apparently expecting to see the actors that portrayed J.R. or Bobby Ewing exit the vehicle. When I could see what was happening, I rolled a window down and told the people "Be patient and we'll sign autographs at the gate as we leave". After a moment of silence, we explained that our group was on tour, had been rescued, and instead of being part of the cast - we were hoping to meet a celebrity or two!

Moving on to west Texas, travelers can see the Palo Duro Canyon area near Amarillo, a very interesting place and at Langtry, you can find Judge Roy Bean's Visitors Center. At Fredericksburg, you can see the Admiral Nimitz Museum, which is the best for those interested in World War II action. Texas has more military facilities than many other states. Central Texas is a beautiful place in the spring time, with various flowers including Bluebonnets, which are the state flower. The bluebonnets are dominant near the Lyndon B. Johnson Ranch; they appear to go on for miles. One special place in South Texas is the Kings Ranch. It is the largest ranch in the state, with more than 800,000 acres and was started by Captain Richard King, in 1853. When we visited the ranch, the employees made and cooked bread for us out on the range and showed us all around.

In Central Texas, near Waco, is the Texas Rangers Hall of Fame. Down between Austin and San Antonio are two of my favorite small cities in Texas: San Marcos and New Braunfels. This is where I spent several months, at Gary A.F.B., which is no longer there. My military experience took me to three places in Texas: Fort Bliss, near El Paso; Fort Hood, near Killeen; and Gary Air Force Base, near San Marcos. The stay at Gary A.F. B. was most pleasant, because of the beautiful surroundings.

Padre Island National Seashores is a great place to spend time in the winter months. We have enjoyed the area from Aransas Pass all the way down to Port Isabel, near Brownsville.

★ Kelly's Perspective & Lessons Learned ★

Several successful business meetings and holidays have taken place in the greater Dallas-Fort Worth area. Highlights include: visits with the publishers of my first book, remarkable shopping in the city where Neiman Marcus began, memorable art museum exhibits, and award-winning dinners to celebrate many important personal and business milestones.

★ Famous People Born in Texas ★

Mary Kay Ash the cosmetics entrepreneur, born in Hot Wells in 1918.

Gene Autry the singer and actor, born in Tioga in 1907.

Carol Burnett the comedienne, born in San Antonio in 1933.

Dwight David Eisenhower the 34th U.S. president and general, born in Denison in 1890.

Larry Hagman the actor, born in Fort Worth in 1931.

Buddy Holly the musician, born in Lubbock in 1936.

Lyndon B. Johnson the 36th U.S. president, born in Stonewall in 1908.

George Jones the singer, born in Saratoga in 1931.

Mary Martin the singer and actress, born in Weatherford in 1913.

Willie Nelson the singer, born in Abbot 1933.

Sandra Day O'Connor the jurist, born in El Paso in 1930.

Roy Orbison the singer, born in Vernon in 1936.

Buck Owens the singer, born in Sherman in 1929.

★ Where Will You Visit? ★

★ What Photos Will You Take? ★

State Capital: Salt Lake City

State Flower: Sego Lily

Population: 2,763,885 (Ranks 34th, as of 2010 Census)

Land Area: 82,169.62 square miles (Ranks 12th)

Population Density: 33.6 persons per square mile (Ranks 45th)

★ Arlie's Insight & Highlights ★

Utah, also known as the "Beehive State", came from the Mormon Word, "Deseret", meaning honeybee and it stands for industry and hard work. The word "Utah" comes from the Ute Indian Tribe that lived in the region, where congress organized it as a territory in 1850. It is speculated that the Spanish may have visited the Grand Canyon area as early as 1540, in the area of what is now southern Utah and Arizona, but historians are uncertain. So it was about 235 years before more Spanish explorers visited the Utah Lake area, but Spain had no interest in starting colonies there. The first Americans to visit were fur traders in the early 1800's. Jim Bridger, a scout is said to be the first white man to see the "Great Salt Lake" during the winter of 1824-25. By 1830, travelers were crossing Utah from Santa Fe, New Mexico going to parts of California.

The Mormons were Utah's first permanent settlers. This religious group (The Church of Jesus Christ of Latter-day Saints) was established by Joseph Smith, in Fayette, New York, in 1830. After Smith's death in 1844, Brigham Young became their leader. The Mormons appeared to be persecuted everywhere they went. They traveled through Ohio, Missouri and Illinois and

did not find the religious freedom they were seeking. In 1846, their leader took a group of his people west and they reached the Great Salt Lake region in 1847, and Young settled there.

When Brigham Young arrived with his party in July of 1847, it is said after seeing the Great Salt Lake he said; "This is the place". This settlement had several years of turbulent times before things were peaceful. At this time (1847), the Utah region belonged to Mexico. The U.S. was fighting the Mexican War (1846-1848). The United States won the war and acquired a large land area from Mexico, which included the much of today's state of Utah. In 1849, the Mormon settlers created the "State of Deseret", and adopted their first constitution and in 1850 Congress established the Utah Territory. The settlers then asked to be admitted to the union, with Brigham Young as the first territorial Governor. Between 1849 and 1895, Utah asked many times to be admitted to the union. Congress refused each time because the Mormons were practicing "polygamy" (one man having two or more wives). In reality only a small number of men had more than one wife.

Flash back to the 1850's and the relations between the Mormons and Indians, they were peaceful at first, but some Indians resented the settlers taking their land. In 1853, Ute Chief Walker led attacks on several Mormon settlements, these attacks were known as the "Walker War", but were settled for a while. In 1865, Ute Chief, Black Hawk led attacks against Mormon settlers, this was known as the Black Hawk War. In this war about 50 Mormons were killed, but in 1867, talks with the Indians settled this with the Ute's going to a reservation. In 1857, a group of Indians and others attacked a party of about 140 travelers passing through Utah. Most of the travelers were murdered. Only some of the children were allowed to live. This was known as "Mountain Meadows Massacre". A man

named John Lee, who took part in the massacre was convicted and executed.

In 1862, congress passed a law forbidding polygamy and during the 1880"s Federal Courts started enforcing laws against polygamy. Hundreds of Mormons were fined and sent to prison. In 1887, a law passed that allowed the U.S. Government to seize church property for other use. In 1890, Wilford Woodruff, the church president advised the Mormons to give up the practice of Polygamy and in October of that year, the church officially prohibited polygamy.

In 1895, Utah submitted the new constitution that outlawed the practice of polygamy and prevented control of a state by any church and Utah was admitted to the union as the 45th state on Jan. 4, 1896.

The geography of Utah, is fairly simple; about half of the state, east and southeast, is part of the Colorado Plateau and the western 30% north to south is the basin and range region. The Northeastern portion is the Rocky Mountains and consist of the Wasatch and Uinta Mountain Ranges, they contain lots of beautiful high peaks and lots of tree cover. West and southwest of the Salt Lake Area is called the "Great Salt Lake Desert".

To the visitor, Utah holds many surprises, it has a great diversity of terrain. One can see tall green mountains and lush valleys, rivers and lakes of many descriptions, but much of the state is arid, dry desert. The basin and range area has streams that terminate into lakes that have no outlet so the water dries-up or evaporates.

The southern half of Utah has more national parks and national monuments than any state we have visited. Some of them have striking and unusual beauty. We have not visited all of them, but where we visited was well worth the time and effort.

In southwest Utah, near Cedar City, is Zion National Park and Bryce Canyon National Park. In the southeastern part of the state is; Canyon-lands National Park, Arches National Park and Capitol Reef National Park. Scattered over the same general area, Utah has several other national monuments, they are; Rainbow Bridge, Cedar Breaks, Natural Bridges and Timpanogos Cave in northern Utah near American Fork. A must see, is the Kennicot open pit copper mine, it's the world's largest, I was awed at this place on our visit there.

Another historic point is at Promontory, were on May 10,1869 , the first U.S. Transcontinental Railroad was completed and Governor Stanford of California drove the final spike, made of gold.

Our travels in Utah, have taken us from one end of the state to the other. In Southern Utah, we have experienced nature's canyons and sculptures while enjoying all the awe-inspiring views of this strange land, it holds certain strange mysteries for me.

Most of Utah's population is located from Provo, north to Logan, near the Idaho border. This is where one finds a lot of history of a determined people (Mormons) who settled this early "promise land".

We enjoyed the Capital grounds and tours of Salt Lake City. We also enjoyed the people of Utah, and found them to be friendly. Another special place we found was Vernal, Utah in the north east corner of the state. We stayed there for a time to enjoy the Dinosaur National Monument. This is a little off the beaten path, but it is a "must-see", this is where one can see the pre-historic creatures, still in the original rocks, a great lesson in geology for the traveler.

A visit to the Great Salt Lake, is unique for one reason, this water is four to five times saltier than any ocean. The visit to the Mormon Temple is also unique, it's the only one of its kind. The visit to Monument Valley is unique, it can be strange and spooky at evening, with many long shadows. Visit all of this interesting state if you can and we hope you enjoy it as much as we did.

★ Kelly's Perspective & Lessons Learned ★

Beyond the famous parks and ski resorts, my favorite areas to explore in the state include Moab as well as Southeastern Utah. You will marvel at the red rock, big sky, mountains, and positive energy of the residence.

★ Famous People Born in Utah ★

Butch Cassidy the outlaw, born in Circleville in 1866.

Anthony Geary the actor, born in Coalville in 1947.

John Gilbert the actor, born in Logan in 1897.

J. Willard Marriott the restaurant and hotel chain founder, born in Marriott in 1900.

Merlin Olsen the football player, born in Logan in 1940.

Donny Osmond the singer, born in Ogden in 1957.

Marie Osmond the singer, born in Ogden in 1959.

Robert Walker the actor, born in Salt Lake City in 1918.

Marie Windsor the actress, born in Marysville in 1919.

James Woods the actor, born in Vernal in 1947.

Loretta Young the actress, born in Salt Lake City in 1913.

★ Where Will You Visit? ★

_____
_____
_____
_____

★ What Photos Will You Take? ★

_____
_____
_____
_____

VERMONT

State Capital: Montpelier

State Flower: Red Clover

Population: 625,741 (Ranks 49th, as of 2010 Census)

Land Area: 9216.7 square miles (Ranks 43rd)

Population Density: 67.9 persons per square mile (Ranks 30th)

★ Arlie's Insight & Highlights ★

Vermont is the memorable green mountain state. When I think of Vermont, I have a mental picture of towns, quite neighborhoods and beautiful white churches with tall steeples in all of these villages. In reality, those mental pictures turned out to be true. The Green Mountains make this state one of the most scenic we have ever traveled.

Vermont is a small state with the Green Mountains running the length north and south of the entire state dividing it into western and eastern sections. Vermont is known for its granite and marble, used for building, memorials and tombs. It is also well supplied with trees and forest for making paper, furniture and other products. The things I remember most from childhood, is the maple syrup, made from the state's maple trees. Vermont is one of the leading states in producing maple syrup and it delivers thousands of gallons each year to global customers.

The geography of Vermont is very complex, it has several different land regions, the two major one's are; the Western New England Uplands and the Green Mountains which cover about 80% of the total land area. The Champlain Valley runs next to Champlain Lake, the Taconic Mountains is a very small area in south west Vermont. In addition, the White Mountains cover a small area of extreme northeaster Vermont.

Vermont, is the only New England state that has no Atlantic coastline, although it has lots of water on its borders. The Connecticut River forms the state's eastern border and Lake Champlain form about half of the border of northwestern Vermont. We had two visits to Vermont, with one in early September, starting the fall color introduction. It seems the bright reds appear first, then the orange and soon the forest is a blaze with all the glorious fall colors.

There is a mystery to me about one of Vermont's former residents. He lived in Arlington, Vermont for over fourteen years, he was and still is one of my favorite Painter/Illustrator of American beauty and culture. His name: Norman Rockwell, who is said not to be a lover of Autumn foliage, to the point where he declined to paint a landscape in the years he lived in Vermont. Having experienced the memorable fall colors, his decision is a mystery for me. Despite this, I collected covers of *The Saturday Evening Post* for many years and I loved them.

Early exploration by Samuel De Champlain, of France, was apparently the first by a white man to explore what is now Vermont and he also claimed the region for France. Fort Drummer was built by Massachusetts settlers in 1724 to protect other western settlers from raids by the French.

The Champlain region became a battle-ground during the French and Indian War of 1754-1763. At the end of the French and Indian War, the treaty gave England control of the Vermont area and much of the rest of North America. Between 1749 and 1763 was a time of "The New Hampshire Grants", England recognized the grants made by New York, but rejected those held by New Hampshire, without New Hampshire paying New York for them. In 1770, a military force called the "Green Mountain Boys" attacked many New York settlers and drove them from Vermont.

At the start of the Revolutionary War, Vermonters were united to fight the British. Ethan Allen and the "Green Mountain Boys" captured Fort Ticonderoga from the British in May, 1775. The battle of Bennington on Aug. 16, 1777 was a major battle of the war and much of it was fought in New York.

In January of 1777, Vermont settlers declared their territory an Independents Republic, called "New Connecticut", and in July of 1777 the area had its first constitution and adopted Vermont as a formal name. Vermont remained as a republic for 14 years. In 1790, Vermont settled the dispute with New York by paying $30,000. New Hampshire also gave up its claim to Vermont, with these improved relations of neighboring states, it cleared the way for Vermont to join the union as the 14th state on March 4, 1791.

During the Civil War, Vermont sent about 34,000 troops to serve with union forces. In 1864, the northern most action oc-

curred when more than 20 confederate soldiers robbed the bank at St. Albans and escaped into Canada with the money.

Vermont has had much turmoil and uncertainty in it's past, however after settling differences with neighboring states it moved on by joining the union. It was also the first territory, after the original 13 Colonies were established, to become part of the United States.

Vermont has many historic and beautiful places to visit. Just about anywhere in this state is very scenic and worth the time effort to see. Some highlights to see are; Bennington Battle Monument at Bennington, Brattleboro Museum and Art Center at Battleboro, Shelburne Museum at Charlotte, Sheldon Museum and Craft Center at Middlebury along with the Vermont Historic Museum at Montpelier.

When you visit New England please tour Vermont. It is delightful to soak-up all the natural beauty that this state has to offer. We hope your visit is as pleasant and colorful as ours was.

★ Kelly's Perspective & Lessons Learned ★

Having been part of the 3 million+ visitors who fall in love with Vermont during the autumn, I vow to return in the near future. In the mean time, if you enjoy history, be sure and look into the historical roadside marker program. Aside from the education and awareness these charming markers give readers a unique insight into the stories of the state's past. With more than 200 markers, you can find the birthplaces of U.S. Presidents, baseball players and founders of world-famous organizations like Cadillac, Lincoln, and Rotary International. In addition, you have an organized roadmap that will lead you to homes of famous authors and luminaries who have influenced our everyday lives. You'll even uncover the origin of technological achievements such as the first ski tow in the U.S.

★ Famous People Born in Vermont ★

Chester Alan Arthur the 21st U.S. president, born in Fairfield in 1829.

Orson Bean the actor, born in Burlington in 1928.

Calvin Coolidge the 30th U.S. president, born in Plymouth in 1872.

John Deere the inventor, born in Rutland in 1804.

John Dewey the philosopher and educator, born in Burlington in 1859.

Richard Morris Hunt the architect, born in Brattleboro in 1827.

William Morris Hunt the painter, born in Bratleboro in 1824.

Elisha Graves Otis the inventor, born in Halifax in 1811.

Moses Pendleton the choreographer, born in Lyndonville in 1949.

Patty Sheehan the golfer, born in Middlebury in 1956.

Joseph Smith the religious leader, born in Sharon in 1805.

Ernest Thompson the actor and writer, born in Bellows Falls in 1949.

★ Where Will You Visit? ★

★ What Photos Will You Take? ★

★ Arlie's Insight & Highlights ★

Virginia, known as "The Mother of Presidents" is one of the most historic of all the states in the union from my view point. Other nicknames include: "Mother of States" and "Old Dominion", which originated over time in Virginia's historic past. Influence for the nicknames comes from the eight U.S. Presidents that were born in Virginia, starting with the countries first: George Washington, next Thomas Jefferson, then followed by half a dozen others including: Presidents' James Madison, James Monroe, William Harrison, John Tyler, Zachary Taylor and Woodrow Wilson who served in office from 1913 through 1921.

Many famous battles were fought on Virginian soil and these historic sites are a must-see for visitors. Yorktown's location is an emotional place for many (myself included) when one sees where the Revolutionary War ended. Another war ended (U.S. Civil War) when General Lee surrendered to General Grant at the Appomattox Court House on April 9, 1865. Other important sites include: George Washington's home in Mount Vernon, Jefferson's residence which he designed in Monticello,

John F. Kennedy's grave as well as the Tomb Of The Unknown Soldier in Arlington National Cemetery.

Four other memorable cities in the surrounding area are: Jamestown, the First Permanent English Settlement in America (1607); Yorktown, which holds Chronicles of the Revolutionary Period from Colonial unrest to the formation of the New Nation; Newport News, the largest U.S. shipyard, where hundreds of (military) ships have been built; and lastly the magnificent Williamsburg, a city that has evoked the days of America's forefathers since its restoration began in the 1920's.

Many things stand out in our visits to the state of Virginia, including certain moments that will be etched in my memory forever. The Yorktown Victory Monument, was authorized by the Continental Congress on October 29, 1781, just after the news of surrender reached Philadelphia. Actual construction began 100 years later and was completed in 1884. The monument was damaged by lightning and a new work replaced it in 1956. This monument is almost 100 ft. in height. While we walked around the battle grounds at Yorktown, I tried to visualize the French

Fleet in Chesapeake Bay, just off shore from the Battleground at Yorktown. As great as General George Washington was, it can't be claimed that they won their independence alone.

Two men: General Rochambeau of the French Army, and Admiral de Grasse of the French Navy, together, and the forces they commanded helped secure a decisive victory for General Washington at this old sea port of Yorktown. This battle not only shortened the war in America, it insured that the United States of America would become a New Nation.

The journey around Williamsburg, Virginia Beach, Newport News, Richmond and Charlottesville took several days, enough time that we had to reschedule our reservations in the Washington D.C. area. The visitor to eastern Virginia must plan plenty of time in their schedule just to see the primary attractions. I will list many that are a must-see for history lovers; Williamsburg, Colonial National Park, Berkeley Plantation, Petersburg National Battlefield and Yorktown, all between Richmond and Norfolk.

The trip out to Charlottesville is a must, here one will find; Monticello, home of Thomas Jefferson, Ash Lawn Highland Home of James Monroe and Michie Tavern Museum. From Richmond north, one may visit several attractions; Scotchtown, home of Patrick Henry, Paramount Kings Dominion, Jackson Shrine, Frederick Battlefield National Military Park and two places near the Potomac River are; George Washington's Birthplace National Monument and Robert E. Lee's Birthplace. While in Alexandria, don't miss Woodlawn, Mount Vernon, and the Manassas National Battlefield Park. We did not get to the Harpers Ferry National Historic Park or Booker T. Washington's National Monument, regretfully. Mount Vernon is a delightful place to visit, we spent lots of time there and I spent some special time down on the Potomac River down the hill from the main house.

In addition to all the historical locations in Virginia, the state has many natural features of land forms and mountain scenery. The state has five basic land regions; beginning on the east side is the Atlantic Costal plains, characterized by lowlands and "tidewater" marshes, the largest of these is the Dismal Swamp in the southeast. The next region to the west is the "Piedmont", the state's largest land region. This region consists of gently rolling plains, averaging about 900 feet in elevation sloping to about 300 ft. on the east. Many rivers flow through this area and the east edge is known as the "Fall Line".

The next region to the west is the "Blue Ridge" mountain area, it runs from North Carolina all the way through Virginia to

Maryland, and has the highest land area in the state. Bordering the Blue Ridge area on the west, is the "Appalachian Ridge and Valley Region"; this area consists of several parallel mountain ridges along most of Virginia's western border.

The largest of these valley areas is the Shenandoah Valley in the north. The fifth land region in Virginia is the "Appalachian Plateau", it's a small, very rugged area in the southwestern part of the state and the plateau has many valuable coal fields.

To me, Virginia's history is very important because what happened there impacted the rest of the nation. Further, I want to share some of the significant dates and happenings in Virginia that reverberated through the colonies. In the beginning, this region was occupied by Native American (Indians) when the English Colonists first arrived. The Powhatan lived on the coastal area and were the first encountered, but many others lived inland on the Piedmont and in the mountain region. Some of the other tribes consisted of the Susquehanna near the upper Chesapeake Bay, the Cherokee in the southwest and the Nottoway in the southeast.

The first Europeans, who settled in the Virginia region were some Spanish Jesuits, in 1570, but the Indians wiped out the settlement in a few months. In 1606, King James I chartered the Virginia Company of London, for colonization purpose and in May, 1607, Colonists sent by this company established the First Permanent English Settlement in America at Jamestown. This colony was led by Captain John Smith and survived many hardships of hunger and cold. In 1609, Smith was injured and had to return to England. The following winter many of the settlers died from starvation. In the spring, many of the Colonists began to leave Jamestown, but they came back after they met the ships of Governor Thomas West, and Lord De La Warr at Hampton Roads. These ships brought supplies and more colonists.

One of the Colonists, John Rolfe, began raising tobacco in 1612, this product could be exported for a profit. The tobacco exporting helped save the colony and gave the people a way to support themselves. In 1614, Mr. Rolfe married Pocahontas, the daughter of Powhatan, Chief of the Indian Tribe around Jamestown. This marriage brought a time of peace between the Indians and the Colonists.

In the year 1619, the Free Colonists were granted land of their own. That same year, 1619, Dutch Trader brought slaves to Virginia for the first time. Also, Americans First Representative Legislature, the House of Burgesses, met in Jamestown. By 1624 Virginia became a Royal Colony.

For the next 100 plus years the Colonies went through turbulent ups and downs. The Kings of England changed many times, the Indians were attacking the Colonist; in 1622 they massacred 347 of them. A group of Colonists (in 1676) led by Nathaniel Bacon rebelled, they resented the Navigation Act imposed by the British. In 1699, the capital was moved from Jamestown to Williamsburg. By 1700, Virginia's population was about 58,000 and was the largest Colony in North America.

The westward expansion of the English Colonists conflicted with the interest of the French and led to the French and Indian War of 1754-1763. In 1775, the second Continental Congress elected George Washington, as Commander and Chief of the Continental Army.

In June, 1776, Virginia became an independent commonwealth when it adopted its first Constitution, with a Declaration of Rights written by George Mason. Patrick Henry was the commonwealth's first Governor and the Capital was moved from Williamsburg to Richmond in 1780. During the Revolutionary War 1775 - 1783, more of Virginians opposed the English than

any other southern colony and the Declaration of Independence was written by Thomas Jefferson, during this period.

Virginia promised in 1781, to give up its claim to the Northwest Territory and it did so in 1784, to the United States. This region was divided into several territories and then into additional States. Until 1789, the 13 original colonies were loosely joined under the Articles of Confederation, but the articles soon proved ineffective. James Mason and other Virginians led in the writing of the Constitution of the United States to replace the articles. Virginia ratified the Constitution on June 25, 1788, and became the 10th state in the union.

During the Civil War period 1861-65, Virginia became a major battle ground, as mentioned earlier, many major battles of this war was fought on Virginia soil. The state seceded from the union in April of 1861, but many westerners in Virginia did not agree to secede. On June 20, 1863, 48 counties of northwest Virginia became the state of West Virginia. Richmond was the capital of the confederacy from May 1861 to April 1865.

After the Civil War, Virginia was readmitted to the union on January 26, 1870. The great and enduring ideas that come from the "Virginia Dynasty", George Washington, Thomas Jefferson, James Monroe and James Madison appeared to have given us a great foundation for a new nation.

Modern day Virginia is one of the most interesting states we have visited, but to enjoy it fully, the visitor must have good maps and a visitor's guide, plus ample time in your schedule to enjoy this state. We discovered several serendipitous side roads on our journey of Virginia.

★ Kelly's Perspective & Lessons Learned ★

Regarding Arlington National Cemetery and on a personal note, I routinely 'thank' all the brave men and women past and present for their military service. My thanks extend to my Dad for his service in the Korean War. Shown here, with a Beechcraft L-23, shortly after cessation of the Korean War in 1953.

Fast forward to a modern day Virginia, which is home to the Pentagon building in Arlington that is one of the largest office buildings in the world, setting on 29 acres, and containing offices for the department of the Army, Air Force, Marine Corps, Navy, and office of the Secretary of Defense.

On a much lighter 1950s note, Virginia designated the northern cardinal as their official state bird. Fitting that one of America's favorite backyard birds would capture this distinctive role.

★ Famous People Born in Virginia ★

Arthur Ashe the tennis player, born in Richmond in 1943.

Pearl Bailey the singer, born in Newport News in 1918.

Warren Beatty the actor, born in Richmond in 1937.

Ella Fitzgerald the jazz singer, born in Newport News in 1917.

William H. Harrison the ninth U.S. president, born in Charles City County in 1773.

Thomas Jefferson the third U.S. president, born in Shadwell in 1743.

Robert E. Lee the Confederate general, born in Stratford in 1807.

James Monroe the fifth U.S. president, born in Westmoreland, in 1758.

James Madison the fourth U.S. president, born in Port Conway, in 1751.

George C. Scott the actor, born in Wise in 1927.

Zachary Taylor the twelfth U.S. president, born in Orange City in 1784.

John Tyler the tenth U.S. president, born in Charles City, in 1790.

George Washington the first U.S. president, born in Westmoreland in 1732.

Woodrow Wilson the twenty-eighth U.S. president, born in Staunton in 1856.

★ Where Will You Visit? ★

★ What Photos Will You Take? ★

State Capital: Olympia

State Flower: Coast Rhododendron

Population: 6,724,540 (Ranks 13th, as of 2010 Census)

Land Area: 66,455.5 square miles (Ranks 20th)

Population Density: 101.2 persons per square mile (Ranks 25th)

★ Arlie's Insight & Highlights ★

Washington, the Evergreen State, is a place of great diversity. This state has mature, thick forests with a great deal of rainfall on the west side and there is no better example of this, than the "Olympic National Park", on the Olympic Peninsula. Our visit to this area was just short of a fantasy world experience. The state's nickname comes from its many species of evergreen trees that include; pines, fir and hemlocks, especially on the western slopes of the Cascade Mountain that run the length of the state from Oregon to British Columbian in Canada.

When western Washington is compared to the area east of the Cascades things are much different. This Columbia Plateau Region desert-like (semiarid) is good for growing crops when the land is irrigated. Some of the special areas are: Walla Walla, Yakima, Wenatchee and the Snake Valley. We have traveled the areas mentioned above and seen the various agriculture crops here, but two specialty crops that stand out in memory are the wheat and apple crops.

Continuing on, the Puget Sound lowland is where Tacoma, Seattle and Olympia are located. This area is where approximately 75% of the residents of Washington live and work. It is also a vibrant area where the shipping, manufacturing and fishing industries occur.

Other land areas of Washington include: the Olympic Mountains in the northwestern region, the Coastal Range in the southwestern corner and the Rocky Mountains in the northeastern corner. These are areas of with rugged terrain that will not support agriculture.

A bit of early history of Washington, reveals that many Native American (Indians) lived in the Washington region before the Europeans appeared. Several tribes lived on each side of the Cascade Mountains, on the east side: Yakima, Spokane, Okanogan, Nez Perce and Cayuse. West of the cascades: The Chinook, Clallam, Clatsop, Nooksack and others that lived on salmon and other species of fish.

The Spanish were some of the first foreigners to explore this Northwest coast area, but no one settled there, until the late 1700's. During this time, Russian fur traders settled in what is now Alaska. The Spanish feared the Russian's would move further south, so they (the Spanish) sent many expeditions there to claim Spain's rights to this area. In 1775, the Spanish did claim the region for Spain. The English also sent explorers to this area, the first was Captain James Cook, in 1778, but no settlements occurred. Another English explorer, Captain Vancouver surveyed the Puget Sound and Georgia Gulf in 1792-1794. One of Vancouver's officers, Peter Puget reached what is now known as the Puget Sound in 1792.

England laid claim to the region based on the exploration of Captain Cook and Captain Vancouver. The Americans also laid claim to this region, based on a Captain Robert Gray's exploration, in 1792, when he explored the mouth of the Columbia River. The most solid claim for the U.S. was the exploration of Lewis and Clark crossing the Rocky Mountains and down the Columbia River to the Pacific Ocean, after the Louisiana Purchase from France. During the early 1800's both the British and American fur traders shared the region. In 1816, an American trader John Jacob Astor set up a fur-trading post at Astoria that is in present day Oregon. This group also founded Fort Okanogan, the first permanent American settlement in what is now Washington State.

After the war of 1812, the U.S. and Britain could not agree on a line to separate their territories west of the Rocky Mountains, so they signed a treaty in 1818 allowing citizens of both countries to trade and settle in this "Oregon Country". During the 1840's large numbers of U.S. citizens began to settle the Oregon Country. During this period the feud between Britain and the U.S. reached a climax. In 1846, President Polk signed a treaty with Britain that set the boundary line at the 49th parallel that is Washington State's present northern border. In 1853, President Fillmore signed a bill creating, the Washington Territory and the Capital was to be at Olympia.

The President appointed Isaac Stevens the first Governor of the New Territory and Stevens attempted to make treaties with the Indians, in order to put them on reservations and create more room for settlers. The coastal Indians signed on to the plan. His efforts, in 1855, to sign treaties with the Plateau Indians failed, leading to a bloody war. A Yakima Chief, Kamiakin, led the warring tribes, but the war ended in 1858, at the battle of "Four Lakes" where the Indians lost. Things settled down and settlers streamed into Washington after 1860's. More settlers came after the completion of the railroad in 1883 and on November 11, 1889, Washington became the 42nd state in the union.

My visits to the state of Washington, began when I was in the forest service in western Montana, we had a visit to a city where you experienced a rushing river through the center of town, Spokane in eastern Washington. My next two visits occurred when I was in the Military Service, this was on the western side of the state at Tacoma and Fort Lewis Washington, before I shipped out to Asia. My next experience to Washington was a very happy occasion, when I returned from Asia (Korea) to receive an Honorable Discharge from the United States Army. From that moment on, all my trips to this state have been for pleasure.

From a different lens and for everyone planning to visit Washington - be prepared to travel several miles and spend plenty of time enjoying the scenic state. Just know that, it's going to be a great adventure. On one of our trips to Washington, we entered the state from Idaho and stayed at Spokane. Here we took photos around the city and went to the city chamber of commerce in search of a tour guide service. They gave us a number to call, so we did, when the guide (driver) arrived he had a pink bus called "Kari Van Tours". This turned-out to be a one-of-a-kind tour, fun, exciting and unusual, because we stopped at all the garage sales in town!? In addition we were able to see the Crosby Alumni House, the Cliff Aerie Estate, the Patsy Clark Mansion and several other landmarks in the city. This was in deed one of those serendipitous side roads of our travels.

As we continued our tour through the state we had a special picnic at Moses Lake in the central Plateau area, we visited Yakima and other cities in the plateau region and finally to the big Mountain, Mt. Rainier National Park. This was truly a breathtaking site, we had to stop often to photograph this mighty mountain. The state has many great mountains, but Rainier happens to be the largest. We visited as close as we could to Mt. St. Helen's while we were staying in Portland, Oregon and that's another story. We journeyed on from Mt. Rainier, to Seattle-Tacoma (SeaTac) area where we stayed for a time.

On a subsequent trip to Washington, we took a tour around Olympic National Park, which is something I had always want-

ed to do. We also stopped at "Hurricane Ridge", spent the night at Fork Washington and enjoyed the coast-line, stayed at Aberdeen and visited Olympia, (The Capital) the following day. This Hwy 101 trip around the park is absolutely beautiful.

There is so much to see in the Seattle area I call it a "must on any visit to Washington". The tours and ferry rides were memorable as we were able to get on and off at different ports, not knowing for sure when we would get back - which turned out to be just one of our adventures. The Space Needle and Monorail are also exciting, these iconic landmarks are from the World Fair of 1962, and they allow you to see mountains and the Puget Sound for miles. We have done so many memorable things in this area, it is hard to narrow down the list of favorites. One suggestion: the Museum of History and Industry, is well worth your time. Out of Seattle to the north, near Mt. Vernon is Hwy 20 to North Cascades National Park and the Ross Lake National recreation area. This whole area is incredibly scenic.

On a visit to Washington, share the rich history of the past and enjoy the beauty of the present by getting good maps along with visitor's guides for the areas you plan to explore. Also remember to take a good camera - as you may have the opportunity to capture enough memories for a lifetime in this remarkable state.

★ Kelly's Perspective & Lessons Learned ★

With visits surrounding business, my focus and experience has been in the greater Seattle area. Even though this is a limited lens, my favorite historic destination is the Fairmont Olympic Hotel. If your itinerary includes Seattle, take time to either stay or visit this luxury hotel, listed on the National Register of Historic Places, located footsteps from the area's finest shops, and a beautiful landmark since opening in 1924.

★ Famous People Born in Washington ★

Carol Channing the actress, born in Seattle in 1921.

Bing Crosby the singer and actor, born in Tacoma in 1903.

Frances Farmer the actress, born in Seattle in 1913.

Bill Gates the software executive, born in Seattle in 1955.

Jimi Hendrix the guitarist, born in Seattle in 1942.

Robert Joffrey the choreographer, born in Seattle in 1930.

Gypsy Rose Lee the entertainer, born in Seattle in 1911.

Kenny Loggins the singer and songwriter, born in Everett in 1948.

Phil Mahre the skier, born in Yakima in 1957.

Francis Scobee the astronaut, born in Cle Elum in 1939.

Smohalla the Indian prophet and chief, born in the Wallula area between 1815 and 1820.

★ Where Will You Visit? ★

★ What Photos Will You Take? ★

WEST VIRGINIA

State Capital: Charleston

State Flower: Rhododendron

Population: 1,852,994 (Ranks 37th, as of 2010 Census)

Land Area: 24,038.2 square miles (Ranks 41st)

Population Density: 77.1 persons per square mile (Ranks 29th)

★ Arlie's Insight & Highlights ★

West Virginia, the mountain state, was part of the state of Virginia before the Civil War. The people were quite different in the eastern settlements of Virginia. These differences were both social and economic The people east of the Allegheny Mountains were more plantation orientated, with trade and tobacco farming, while the settlers west of the Allegheny Mountains were fewer and relied on livestock and food crops. As early as 1776, the people of the west sent petition to the Continental Congress asking for a separate government. During the Civil War (1861-65) the counties of Western Virginia refused to secede with Virginia and organized a separate government and remained in the union. West Virginia, with its separate government, became the 35th state on June 20, 1863.

The extreme rugged terrain of West Virginia, gives the state its nickname, The Mountain State. West Virginia geography, is much the same state wide, but it has two major regions; the Appalachian Plateau covers about 70% of the western part of the state, while the Appalachian Ridge and Valley Region covers the entire eastern portion, except a small part known as the "Blue Ridge" area.

The very early history of the region was occupied by Indians known as the "Mound Builders" and they disappeared long before the first white men arrived in the 1670's. Burial mounds are still visible in the Ohio and Kanawha River Valleys.

During the Civil War, history tells us that the Confederate troops positioned in the Shenandoah Valley, raided parts of West Virginia and the town of Romney changed hands more than 50 times. In 1859, John Brown and his men raided the federal arsenal at Harpers Ferry, at this point, disputes over slavery had reached a climax. After the war started, Virginia had to choose sides, after April 1861. At that time West Virginia joined the union (June 20, 1863) it had a population of about 380,000 people, including 15,000 slaves. This new state sent about 30,000 men to the union army and also more than 8,000 went to the Confederate Military. Many battles were fought the first year of the war and after a series of defeats in 1861-62, Confederate Forces stopped fighting to capture land west of Allegheny Mountains. At the end of the Civil War (1865) Virginia asked West Virginia to reunite with it but West Virginia declined the offer.

Modern day West Virginia, is a great producer of coal, it produces more than most states in that region, except Kentucky. The growth of manufacturing industries and tourism gives much hope to increase the economies of the population and the state. Probably the only thing that has not changed over time is the terrain. The "Mountain State" has a great deal of scenery for visitors, we have traveled the state only twice, once in the northern part and once in the southern portion and the mountains are memorable.

In our travels, we have visited only three major cities in West Virginia. Morgan Town is the north, Charleston the Capital and Huntington in the southwest. Some of the places we would like to visit are: Harpers Ferry National Historic Park, River Underground, Seneca Rocks, Seneca Caverns and the birth place of Pearl Buck at Hillsboro, this lady must have been very special to win the Pulitzer Prize in 1932 and win a second Nobel Prize in 1938. After reading more on this fascinating author, I learned that she had written more than 100 books. Our relatives told us of their visit to Moundsville, where they enjoyed a visit to the "Fostoria Glass Museum", this would be a must-see if one collects Fostoria.

It would be another adventure for us to see the sights mentioned above and have the time to enjoy the trip. Five of these locations are located in the eastern part, known as the Appalachian Ridge of West Virginia, which we missed on previous journeys.

★ Famous People Born in West Virginia ★

George Brett the baseball player, born in Glendale in 1953.

Pearl S. Buck the author, born in Hillsboro in 1892.

Phyllis Curtin the soprano, born in Clarksburg in 1921.

Joanne Dru the actress, born in Logan in 1922.

Thomas Stonewall Jackson the Confederate general, born in Clarksburg in 1824.

John S. Knight the publisher, born in Bluefield in 1894.

Don Knotts the actor, born in Morgantown in 1924.

Peter Marshall the TV host, born in Huntington in 1926.

Kathy Mattea the country musician, born in South Charleston in 1959.

Mary Lou Retton the gymnast, born in Fairmont in 1968.

Eleanor Steber the soprano, born in Wheeling in 1914.

Lewis L. Strauss the naval officer and scientist, born in Charleston in 1896.

Chuck Yeager the test pilot and Air Force general, born in Myra in 1923.

Steve Yeager the baseball player, born in Huntington in 1948.

★ **Where Will You Visit?** ★

_____
_____
_____
_____

★ **What Photos Will You Take?** ★

_____
_____
_____
_____

State Capital: Madison

State Flower: Wood Violet

Population: 5,686,986 (Ranks 20th, as of 2010 Census)

Land Area: 54,157.8 square miles (Ranks 25th)

Population Density: 105 persons per square mile (Ranks 23rd)

★ Arlie's Insight & Highlights ★

Wisconsin, also known as the Badger State, is a great producer of dairy products that includes milk, butter and many famous cheeses. The Wisconsin nickname, the Badger State, came from early lead miners that lived in caves, dug from the hillsides. This reminded other residents of the Badgers that dug similar holes for their homes and the name stuck. The state's

name, Wisconsin, is said to be an Indian name, with multiple meanings: Wild Rice Country, and Homeland, both appropriate based on the past when Native Americans lived in the region.

In more recent times, Wisconsin has become known as one of the most "progressive' state in the union. Starting several economic and social programs such as: The first Kindergarten at Watertown, in 1856, by Margaretha Schurz, the first hydro-electric plant in the country built on the Fox River, in 1882. Cheese making was introduced commercially by settlers from New York about 1845, workers compensation, 1911, teacher's pension, 1911, minimum wage laws, 1913, old age pensions, 1931 and unemployment compensation in 1932. The state of Wisconsin has a lot of "First's" in its history.

Wisconsin is a beautiful place to visit, but it was my research of Muskie fishing that convinced me to go there and see for myself. I had collected, Sports Afield, Outdoor Life and Field and Stream magazines for many years and read all the Muskie stories.

Further research by phone, convinced me that northern Wisconsin was the best place to try for some great Muskie fishing. The next step was to acquire good maps of the area and good lodging. We found good lodging at "The Pointe" resort and hotel on beautiful Lake Minocqua. I could never describe the wonderful amenities and great services they provided, including a boat at the private dock. We acquired several U.S. Geological Topo maps of Oneida and Vilas counties to enhance our understanding of the area. This location on Lake Mihocqua was most ideal, it allowed us to travel and fish four different Lakes, without removing our boat from the water. These lakes were; Lake Minocqua, Lake Kawaguesaga, Mid Lake and Tomahawk Lake. Some of these lakes had good Muskie, northern pike and walleye fishing. We Did It All! One day I told my wife she had a strike, she came running and the rod was gone into the lake and she went into the Lake after it, but I had to retrieve her and the rod! We had several exciting encounters in northern Wisconsin and we did hire a guide on each of our three fishing trips to the state.

We made a combination trip of our four visits to Wisconsin, then we made a special trip to get an over-view of the state, beginning at St. Paul, Minnesota to Eau Claire, then north to Hayward, where we found the National Fresh Water Fishing Hall Of Fame.

On this special overview trip, we traveled from Hayward, north to Superior Wisconsin, then east along Lake Superior to Ashland, then southeast to Rhinelander, then journeyed on south to Wausau, Stevens Point, Portage and on to Madison, the capital, where we stayed a while. From Madison, we journeyed to Milwaukee, Wisconsin's largest city, and then on south to Racine and Kenosha, before exiting the state into Illinois. On the trek through Wisconsin, we encountered several serendipitous side roads, always a pleasure to discover.

The part of Wisconsin that we have not traveled is part of the Great Lakes Plaines area around Oshkosh, Appleton and the Green Bay area, this could be another trip.

On this special trip from one end to the other of Wisconsin, revealed much about the geography of this state. It has five major land areas; the Superior Upland, the Central Plain, the Western upland, the Great Lakes Plains and a smaller region known as the Lake Superior Lowlands. The superior upland covers most of northern Wisconsin, sloping gradually toward the south. The Central Plains runs through the central part of the state and the Wisconsin river has carved a scenic gorge known as the Wisconsin Dells. The western uplands, has many bluffs of sandstone beauty along the Mississippi River. The Great Lakes Plains runs from the Green Bay area south to Illinois, and it contains good agricultural land for growing crops.

Regardless of where we traveled in Wisconsin, there was some magnetic attraction to Wisconsin's north woods, more specifically the Oneida and Vilas counties. This is where we spent three unforgettable trips. One experience of nature I must share with the reader; the encounter with the "Loons". My first experience with loons, occurred in northwest Montana when I was in the U.S. forest service, but loons were rare in that region of Montana. I had not heard the call of this bird again - until our visit to northern Wisconsin. Here, the loons appeared to be numerous. We stayed up late many nights fishing and listening to the loons do their special communications. The call of

this bird is a wailing and mysterious sound that makes me feel an unknown connection to the distant past. The wailing call of a loon, to me represents everything that's wild! The adult loon has four types of calls; the Yodel, Hoot, Wail and the Tremolo (a trembling sound).

One day while resting in the lounge at "The Pointe Resort", I met a doctor from out-of-state and I was sharing my thoughts about the loons and he said, "That's Interesting. We've have been using recordings of the loons, along with other sounds of nature, in our work at the prison re-hab center back in Minnesota". We had a long interesting visit and shared our thoughts on the communication of the loons.

On one of our outings, fishing for Muskie, I hooked a nice sized fish and got it in, when our guide started to take the hooks out (without pliers) the fish cut his thumb to the bone. We used my hankie tied tightly around his thumb as a temporary bandage. This was not the experience we expected, but we still had great day fishing, we released the fish back into the wild. All of our fishing trips to northern Wisconsin were productive, we caught at least one Muskie on each trip, plus Northern Pike and other species. There are a myriad of lakes in Oneida and Vilas counties that provide excellent Muskie and Walleye fishing. We caught a Muskie in Lake St. Germain and another Muskie in Lake Arbor Vitae in Vilas County.

All of this area has some left-over signs of the Glaciers that once covered the region. At some road-side parks in Wisconsin, the state has some signs and illustrations of land forms, usually unfamiliar to most travelers with names like Kettle Lakes, Kames and Eskers, all tell-tale signs of the Ice Ages.

A bit of past history for the state of Wisconsin would be appropriate to see how this state arrived at State-hood. In 1763, the English received the Wisconsin Region from France by the Treaty of Paris (This was the end of the French and Indian War). In 1783, Wisconsin became a part of the United States. Many years later (in 1836) Congress created the Wisconsin Territory.

Wisconsin had some periods of rapid growth in its past. In 1840, the state had a mere 30,000 white people living in the state. By 1850, the population had exploded to 305,000. New comers arrived from parts of the United Stated and other European Countries and by May 29,1848 Wisconsin had become the 3oth state in the Union.

Wisconsin may carry the title of "America's Dairyland", but it has so much more to offer. My visits there will be tattooed in memory forever. I will always want to return to Wisconsin for the Great Muskie Fishing, but the loons may entice me back with their haughty call of the wild.

★ Kelly's Perspective & Lessons Learned ★

My first visit to Wisconsin was memorable, as I arrived in the cockpit of a regional jet aircraft while occupying the jumpseat. Although monitoring the engine performance was my priority during the flight, the highlight had to be seeing Oshkosh. Having heard so much about this spirited city, I was pleased that our flight path took us so close to the site which hosts over 500,000 people and 10,000 planes during the annual Oshkosh fly-in convention. A career highlight!

On a culinary note, I was able to visit a few of the award-winning Wisconsin Cheese Factories before business meetings began. After discovering that Wisconsin produces over 35 percent of our nation's cheese – I had to go and experience it for myself. What I learned is that many factories welcome visitors, several offer tours, and I found the cheese to be amazing.

★ Famous People Born in Wisconsin ★

Dr. Anne Carlsen the educator, born in Grantsburg in 1915.

William Defoe the actor, born in Appleton in 1955.

Tyne Daly the actress, born in Madison in 1946.

August Derleth the author, born in Sauk City in 1909.

Chris Farley the actor, born in Madison in 1964.

Zona Gale the author, born in Portage in 1874.

Woody Herman the band leader, born in Milwaukee in 1913.

Harry Houdini the magician, born in Appleton in 1874.

Liberace the pianist, born in West Allis in 1919.

Allen Ludden the TV host, born in Mineral Point in 1917.

Fredric March the actor, born in Racine in 1897.

Jackie Mason the comedian, born in Sheboygan in 1931.

The Ringling Brothers, Charles (1863) and John (1866), the circus entrepreneurs, born in Baraboo

Pat O'Brien the actor, born in Milwaukee in 1899.

Georgia O'Keeffe the painter, born in Sun Prairie in 1887.

Amy Pietz the actress, born in Oak Creek in 1969.

Tom Snyder the newscaster, born in Milwaukee in 1936.

Spencer Tracy the actor, born in Milwaukee in 1900.

Orson Welles the actor and producer, born in Kenosha in 1915.

Laura Ingalls Wilder the author, born in Pepin in 1867.

Frank Lloyd Wright the architect, born in Richland Center in 1867.

Bob Uecker the baseball player, born in Milwaukee in 1934.

Les Paul the musician, born in Waukesha in 1915.

★ Where Will You Visit? ★

★ What Photos Will You Take? ★

State Capital: Cheyenne

State Flower: Indian Paintbrush

Population: 563,626 (Ranks 50th, as of 2010 Census)

Land Area: 97,093.1 square miles (Ranks 9th)

Population Density: 5.8 persons per square mile (Ranks 49th)

★ Arlie's Insight & Highlights ★

When I think of Wyoming, the first mental picture that comes to mind is the Teton Mountains of western Wyoming. This chain of mountains is one long series of tree-less peaks and if one has seen most of the Rocky Mountains, you know this is a unique series. I love the scenery and beauty that surrounds the Teton Region. Don't misunderstand what I have just related about the Tetons, Wyoming has many other great mountain ranges. I will mention the ones I have visited personally: the Absaroka Range, just east of Yellowstone National Park, the Bighorn Mountains, the Bear Lodge Mountains in the northeastern corner of the state, the Wind River Range, the Salt River Range, the Medicine Bow Mountains and the Laramie Mountains, near Cheyenne, the Capital. I have enjoyed most of the Mountainous Regions of Wyoming. Fishing is one of my favorite sports and I found it in Wyoming.

This State has some important "Firsts" in its history. The world's first National Park, Yellowstone (1872). Wyoming, also known as "The Equality State", the women were the first in the country to vote, the first to hold public office, the first to serve on juries and in 1870, Esther Morris, became the Country's first woman Justice of-the-peace. In 1924, Wyoming elected the first woman governor, Mrs. Nellie Taylor Ross. We don't want to forget that in 1906, President Theodore Roosevelt made the "Devils Tower" the First National Monument.

The first people to live in what is now Wyoming, were Indian people as far back as 11,000 years ago, they were hunters. Later, when French trappers arrived (1700's) there were several native American (Indian) tribes in the region. When the white Europeans arrived, they found; Bannock, Arapaho, Blackfeet, Cheyenne, Nez Perce, Sioux, Utes and others living in the Wyoming Region. The Unites States bought most of this region from France as part of the "Louisiana Purchase," in 1803. In 1807, John Coulter was the first white man to discover the Geysers of the Yellowstone area and in 1812, a group of Oregon Fur Traders, led by Robert Stuart discovered what became known as "South Pass". This route became the best way for pioneers traveling to the west.

During the 1820's and 1830's the fur trade was highly organized, with trappers and traders of certain goods and supplies meeting on a regular basis. The traders swapped food, ammunition and other supplies for furs. This exchange was led by Captain Ben de Bonneville, the same party that discovered oil in Wyoming in 1833. In 1834 two traders, William Sublette and Robert Campbell, established Fort Williams in eastern Wyoming. The fort, was later named Fort Laramie that became the first permanent trading post in the state. Jim Bridger, a famous trapper and guide, founded Fort Bridger in southwest Wyoming in 1843. In 1842-43, Lieutenant John Fremont, was exploring in the Wind River Mountain Range, guided by the famous Scout, Kit Carson.

Congress voted to establish forts along the Oregon Trail in 1846, to protect the settlers moving west. Fort John, was renamed by the army and called Fort Laramie. This entire region was part of many territories, before it was Wyoming. These territories were; Louisiana, Nebraska, Missouri, Oregon, Washington, Idaho, Utah, Dakota and two countries earlier, Spain and Mexico.

It was not until 1868, that congress created the territory of Wyoming. In the mean-time, during the 1840's and 1850's, newcomers (pioneers) were heading west on three famous trails; the Oregon Trail, the California Trail and the Mormon Trail. All these trails went through (south pass) the easiest way through the mountains. It's unusual that all these settlers passed through this land, but very few stayed in Wyoming. The native Americans (Indians) watched this activity happen. One of the greatest migrations (movements) in history, happened right in their hunting grounds and the white settlers caused raging prairie fires, which passed diseases that killed many of the native Indians. The natives were incensed over this blatant aggression of their homeland and the angry warriors began to attack the wagon trains. The Indians not only raided the wagons, but fought the soldiers sent to protect the pioneer travelers. In 1854, near Fort Laramie, Lieutenant Grattan and 29 soldiers were killed. The Plains Indians were good horsemen and brave warriors. The United Tribes were a formidable force, even against the U.S. Army.

In the 1860's gold was discovered in Montana and settlers moved up the Bozeman Trail to Montana. This trail went right

through the prime Indian lands, so to keep this trail (Bozeman) open the Army built "Fort Phil Kearny" in north central Wyoming in 1866. The Sioux disliked the fort, so Chief Red Cloud put war parties all around the place and it was called the "Circle of Death". During the first six months 150 men were killed. Captain Fetterman and 81 of his troops died in one battle. Finally in 1868 a treaty was signed (without much meaning) but the army did give up this fort and left northeastern Wyoming to the Indians. A troubled peace with the Indians lasted until 1874 when gold was discovered in the Black Hills, this area (Black Hills) was sacred to the Indians.

White men by the hundreds violated the treaties by moving into the area in search for gold. The result was war with the Sioux and Cheyenne that had won two major battles in nearby Montana with U.S. Troops. After these major encounters however, the Indian forces broke up and went to Canada to avoid more U.S. Troops and many Indians were moved to reservations.

Serious Indian fighting ended after 1876, and the settlers found peace in most of Wyoming, except for feuding and fighting among the large ranchers, sheep ranchers, small ranchers and farmers (sod-busters). Ranching did support the new territory's economy, because of large numbers of longhorn cattle driven up from Texas.

It was July 10, 1890 when Wyoming became the 44th state in the union. The visitor to modern-day Wyoming will find that mining of coal and drilling of oil and gas continues to be the major source of economic growth in this state. A brief flash back in history tells us that Wyoming's mineral industry began long before it was a territory. In 1833, the Bonneville Party greased its wagon axles where oil seeded from the ground in the Wind River Basin and Jim Bridger sold oil at his fort, and the pioneers mixed it with flour to use as axle grease for their wagons.

Camping with an "RV" in Wyoming is great to check-out the many camping places available for fishing and sight-seeing. We have done most of the state with a camping trailer and motel stays. One of the most remote trips was out of Meeteese, where we had a federal oil lease, near a small place called Pitchfork. One of the most fun places I recall was just out of Jackson south on the Snake River where we rafted near Alpine. This was a breathtaking experience. We did the; Roller Coaster Ride, the Big Kahuna, the Rope, Lunch Counter, the Champagne "River of Bubbly" and The Holy City Hell's Half-mile, you just don't forget these things! We took the ride to the top of the Tetons, and took lots of photos, it was an out-of-sight experience. We have Trekked all over the Yellow Stone National Park's old faithful Geyser, the Fountain Paint Pot, the falls and much more.

We had a great visit to Cody, Wyoming and the Buffalo Bill Historic Center, don't miss this one it's a must-see. Our trip to Pinedale and fishing in this area was special. We stayed in Lander for a while, and visited the grave of Sacajawrea nearby. In Thermopolis, one will find the world's largest mineral Hot Springs. We camped at a nice place out from "Nowhere" near the town of Alcova where we fished and had a deer in camp that I called the "Deer Without Fear", you could not scare that deer out of your way!

We journeyed to far northeastern Wyoming to visit the Devils Tower National Monument, the one used in the movie; "The Close Encounters of the third kind (1977)," although we enjoyed the area - we did not climb the tower! We have traveled to many of the historic sites in Wyoming, but still many we have not seen. Some special ones in history are; Ft. Bridger in southwestern Wyoming, and Ft. Laramie in southeastern Wyoming. Several are located in the north central area, around Buffalo and Sheridan; Ft. Phil Kearny, Trails End State Historic site, Connor Battlefield St. Historic Site and Medicine Wheel National Historic site, near Lovell. South central Wyoming sites include: Independence Rock site, South Pass City site and the Whitman Monument.

There is much to do and although the distance is far, it is a great pleasure to explore Wyoming.

★ Kelly's Perspective & Lessons Learned ★

While growing up, I remember my mother saying that Jackson Hole, Wyoming was one of the most beautiful places she had been. Two years ago, I went to a family reunion with my husband and we made to journey to see for ourselves. She was right.

The Grand Teton range and sweeping Snake River are just the beginning of your list of landmarks to see. With hundreds of square miles of prime land, the area surrounding Jackson Hole is a sanctuary for elk, bald eagles, bison, mountain lions, and wolves together with many other creatures that avid photographers spend a life time searching for.

★ Famous People Born in Wyoming ★

John Buck the baseball player, born in Kemmerer in 1980.

Lynne Cheney the author, born in Casper in 1941.

Velma Linford the writer, born in Afton in 1907.

Dana Perino the politician, born in Evanston in 1972.

Jackson Pollock the painter, born in Cody in 1912.

Alan K. Simpson the senator, born in 1931.

Chief Washakie the chief of the Shoshone, born near Wakemap in 1798.

James G. Watt the secretary of the Interior, born in Lusk in 1938.

★ Where Will You Visit? ★

_____

_____

_____

_____

★ What Photos Will You Take? ★

_____

_____

_____

_____

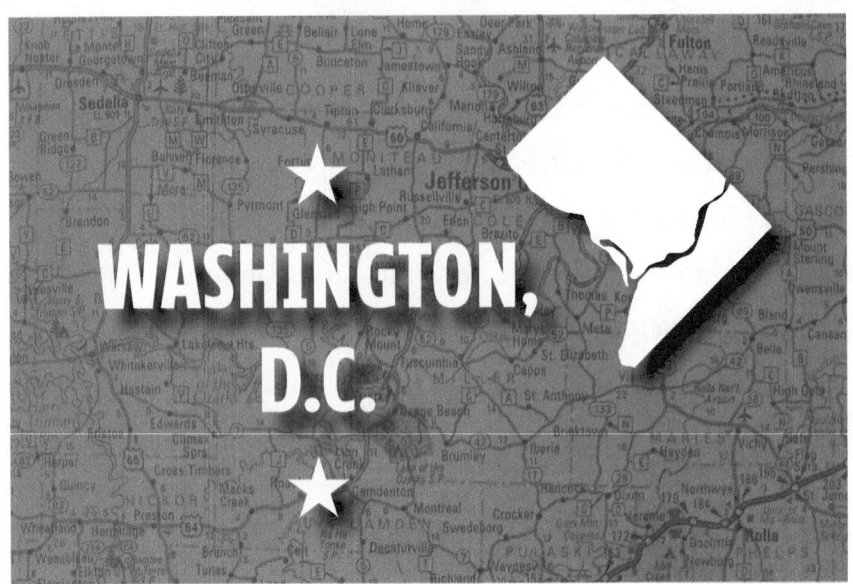

WASHINGTON, D.C.

★ Arlie's Insight & Highlights ★

Before we started the trip to the U.S. Capital, a friend who is a retired Colonel told me of a study about the Washington, D.C. sites and museums. He said that to read all the plaques, instructions, and historical data would take thirty-eight years! There are dozens of important buildings and monuments all over this city.

To get a good overview, a map and visitor's guide is essential. Sources are many and examples include the American Automobile Association (AAA) and Rand McNally for starters.

A little research into the history of Washington, D.C. will reveal many interesting things. The city is located between Maryland and Virginia on the bank of the Potomac River. Unlike most American cities, Washington, D.C. was designed before it was built.

According to history, President Washington chose the location in 1791 and hired a French engineer to make the plans for the future city. The U.S. Capital was located in Philadelphia at the time (1790-1800).

In the year 1800, Washington, D.C. replaced Philadelphia as the Capital of the United States. Unlike other large American cities, you will not see any skyscrapers in Washington, D.C. because the heights of buildings are set by the law for this city.

When we arrived in Washington, D.C. we stayed in a hotel next to the Watergate Hotel. This is a group of buildings (a complex) near the Kennedy Center. The term Watergate is famous now because of the 1972 break-in by some campaign workers for President Nixon who broke into the Democratic Headquarters.

We took bus tours, walking tours, and automobile tours. At night we could look into the activities of the Watergate Hotel and everything looked peaceful (no break-ins).

The visit to D.C. was inspiring and each day was an adventure. We began to realize how amazing this place is. One of the first sites to visit was the Capitol on Capitol Hill. The building has more than 500 rooms. Some are lined with sculptures, carvings, beautiful paintings, and all sorts of great art. It is regal inside and out. The Rotunda Dome was a favorite.

The Supreme Court Building is so regal it's something you might see in old Athens, Greece.

As you go west from the Capitol, the visitor will encounter the National Mall; this is a long, narrow piece of land, with buildings on both sides. Many of the Smithsonian museums are found along this stretch of the "Mall". For those who enjoy art from all over the world, this is a special place to hang out for days.

Just west of the mall one can see the tallest structure in Washington, D.C., the Washington Monument. It is a structure more than 500 feet tall. Inside the Monument one can use the elevator to go to the top, where one can look out tiny windows and see most of the city. This monument was dedicated to the memory of President Washington. Farther west from the Washington Monument is a place called the Reflecting Pool and at the west end of it stands the magnificent Lincoln Memorial. Inside the Memorial is a statue of Lincoln seated in a chair. The outside has 36 columns, one for each state that existed when President Lincoln was killed.

Going southeast from the Lincoln Memorial, we saw another very famous memorial that honors Thomas Jefferson. This is a circular structure of white marble topped with a beautiful dome and a statue of Jefferson stands inside. The Jefferson Memorial is located on the south edge of the Tidal Basin, well-known for many of the Japanese cherry trees that bloom so beautifully in the spring. April is a good month to see this wonderful sight.

North of Washington Monument and at the west end of Pennsylvania Avenue, at number 1600, we find the White House. The White House is the home of the President and has been for every president except President Washington.

The White House has more than 130 rooms but only a very few of those rooms are open to the public. Those rooms were the Green Room, Red Room, Blue Room, East Room and the State Dining Room. Visitors are not allowed where the President lives and works.

Among other points of interest, and one in particular, is the Ford Theatre. This is the Playhouse where President Lincoln was shot, but this is not where he died. The Peterson house,

across the street from the Ford Theatre is where he passed away. We photographed both of the locations and it was very sad.

There are many places outside of Washington D.C. proper to visit as well. While still in the D.C. area, there is the beautiful setting of the Kennedy Center for Performing Arts. It is on the east bank of the Potomac River just north of the Lincoln Memorial. Large crowds visit this place to honor the memory of John F. Kennedy, the President for whom it is dedicated. As we travel west across the Potomac River, we find the Pentagon Building. It is the Department of Defense Headquarters and considered one of the largest office buildings in the world. On the same side of the river (west side) we find the very large Arlington National Cemetery, also in Virginia.

This cemetery contains the graves of many thousands of soldiers who served in the United States Military Services. It also contains the Tomb of the Unknown Soldier. Here we find the grave of President Kennedy, where a flame burns day and night. Another special place nearby is the Iwo Jima statue, also called the Marine Corps War Memorial. It shows five servicemen raising the flag on the island of Iwo Jima during World War II. When we observed this statue, it was a very emotional set of moments, as I reflected on my own personal military experience.

As we travel out from the city to the south, approximately 20 miles, we find Mount Vernon, on the west bank of the Potomac River. This was the private residence and estate of George Washington. This is where the Father of our Country lived, and where some of his belongings and grave remain today.

As we visited the estate, I walked down to the river, stood on the bank, gazed across the river for several minutes, wondering how many times President Washington may have stood in this very spot, looking across the Potomac River and what he was thinking 235 years before I was here.

When we departed Washington, D.C., I thought what a short and intense education this was. We have thoughts and memories of this remarkable destination that will remain with us forever.

★ Kelly's Perspective & Lessons Learned ★

One of my favorite cities in the nation, Washington D.C. is the destination that may inspire a future book. In the mean time, highlights follow.

Historic, majestic, and stunningly beautiful, the White House, the Capitol, and the Supreme Court guard the heart of Washington D.C. They are all, favorite destinations when combined with a stay at the sophisticated and charming Willard Hotel.

★ Famous People Born in Washington D.C. ★

Kevin Durant the basketball player, born in 1988.

Albert Gore Jr. the 45th U.S. vice president, born in 1948.

Samuel L. Jackson the actor, born in 1948.

Raven Goodwin the actress, born 1992.

Andrew Luck the football player, born 1989.

Alyson Hannigan the actress, born in 1974.

Katherine Heigl the actress, born in 1978.

Marvin Gaye the singer, born in 1939.

Mya the singer, born in 1979.

Goldie Hawn the actress, born in 1945.

Christopher Meloni the actor, born in 1961.

Stephen Colbert the TV show host, born in 1964.

John F. Kennedy Jr. the entrepreneur, born in 1960.

Duke Ellington the pianist, born in 1899.

Tim Gunn, the TV host, born in 1953.

Vernon Davis the football player, born in 1984.

★ Where Will You Visit? ★

★ What Photos Will You Take? ★

★ APPENDIX ★

State & Capital City	State Bird	State Flower	State Tree
Alabama (Montgomery)	Yellow Hammer	Yellow Hammer	Camellia
Alaska (Juneau)	Yellow Ptarmigan	Forget-me-not	Sitka Spruce
Arizona (Phoenix)	Cactus Wren	Saguaro	Paloverde
Arkansas (Little Rock)	Mockingbird	Apple Blossom	Pine
California (Sacramento)	California Valley Quail	Golden Poppy	California Redwood
Colorado (Denver)	Lark Bunting	Rocky Mountain Columbine	Blue Spruce
Connecticut (Hartford)	Robin	Mountain Laurel	White Oak
Delaware (Dover)	Bluehen Chicken	Peach Blossom	American Holly
Florida (Tallahassee)	Mockingbird	Orange Blossom	Sabal Palm
Georgia (Atlanta)	Brown Thrasher	Cherokee Rose	Live Oak
Hawaii (Honolulu)	Hawaiian Goose	Hibiscus	Kukui
Idaho (Boise)	Mountain Bluebird	Syringer	Western White Pine
Illinois (Springfield)	Cardinal	Native Violet	White Oak
Indiana (Indianapolis)	Cardinal	Peony	Tulip Tree
Iowa (Des Moines)	Eastern Goldfinch	Wild Rose	Oak
Kansas (Topeka)	Western Meadowlark	Sunflower	Cottonwood
Kentucky (Frankfort)	Kentucky Cardinal	Goldenrod	Tulip Poplar
Louisiana (Baton Rouge)	Brown Pelican	Magnolia	Bald Cypress
Maine (Augusta)	Chickadee	White Pine Cone	White Pine
Maryland (Annapolis)	Baltimore Oriole	Black-eyed Susan	White Oak
Massachusetts (Boston)	Chickadee	Mayflower	American Elm
Michigan (Lansing)	Robin	Apple Blossom	White Pine
Minnesota (St. Paul)	Common Loon	Pink and White Lady's Slipper	Norway Pine
Mississippi (Jackson)	Mockingbird	Magnolia	Magnolia
Missouri (Jefferson City)	Blue Bird	Hawthorne	Flowering Dogwood
Montana (Helena)	Western Meadowlark	Bitteroot	Ponderosa Pine
Nebraska (Lincoln)	Western Meadowlark	Goldenrod	Cottonwood

State & Capital City	State Bird	State Flower	State Tree
Nevada (Carson City)	Mountain Bluebird	Sagebrush Single-leaf	Pinon
New Hampshire (Concord)	Purple Finch	Purple Lilac	White Birch
New Jersey (Trenton)	Eastern Goldfinch	Purple Violet	Red Oak
New Mexico (Santa Fe)	Road Runner	Yucca Flower	Nut Pine
New York (Albany)	Bluebird	Rose	Sugar Maple
North Carolina (Raleigh)	Cardinal	Flowering Dogwood	Pine
North Dakota (Bismarck)	Western Meadowlark	Wild Prairie Rose	American Elm
Ohio (Columbus)	Cardinal Scarlet	Carnation	Buckeye
Oklahoma (Oklahoma City)	Scissor-tailed Flycatcher	Mistletoe	Redbud
Oregon (Salem)	Western Meadowlark	Oregon Grape	Douglas Fir
Pennsylvania (Harrisburg)	Ruffed Grouse	Mountain Laurel	Hemlock
Rhode Island (Providence)	Rhode Island Red	Violet	Red Maple
South Carolina (Columbia)	Carolina Wren	Carolina Jessamine	Palmetto
South Dakota (Pierre)	Ring-necked Pheasant	American Pasque Flower	Black Hills Spruce
Tennessee (Nashville)	Mockingbird	Iris Tulip	Poplar
Texas (Austin)	Mockingbird	Bluebonnet	Pecan
Utah (Salt Lake City)	Seagull	Sego Lily	Blue Spruce
Vermont (Montpelier)	Hermit Thrush	Red Clover	Sugar Maple
Virginia (Richmond)	Cardinal	Flowering Dogwood	Flowering Dogwood
Washington (Olympia)	Willow Goldfinch	Coast Rhododendron	Western Hemlock
West Virginia (Charleston)	Cardinal	Rhododendron	Sugar Maple
Wisconsin (Madison)	Robin	Wood Violet	Sugar Maple
Wyoming (Cheyenne)	Meadowlark	Indian Paintbrush	Cottonwood

★ BIBLIOGRAPHY ★

American Automobile Association, 1000 AAA Drive, Heathrow, Florida

America From the Road, Readers Digest Association Inc., 1982

American's Great Outdoors, The Outdoor Writers Association of America. 1976

American Sightseeing, 17 E. Monroe St., Chicago, Illinois

Gray Line, Worldwide Tour Service, 1835 Gaylord St., Denver, Colorado

National Geographic Society Headquarters, Washington D.C., Founded, January, 1888

North American Wildlife, Readers Digest Association, Inc., 1982

Physical Geography (Third Edition) John Wiley and Sons, Inc., New York, 1969

Presidents of the United States, Field Enterprises Education Corp., 1976

Scenic Wonders of America, Readers Digest Association, Inc., 1973

The Road Atlas Easy-To-Read, Rand McNally, 2001

World Atlas 1890, Rand McNally and Company, copyright 1890

The American Pageant, Original Publisher, *A History of the Republic*, by Thomas Bailey, 1956

★ About the Authors ★

Arlie Isley has worked for the U.S. Forest Service, AT&T, and was a member of the U.S. Army. His time in the army enabled him to be a world traveler to places such as Korea and Japan, while his early retirement from AT&T gave him many opportunities to travel throughout the United States.

Growing up in Geary, Oklahoma Arlie attended Oklahoma University, Oklahoma State University, and Central State University, completing degrees in Economics and Geography.

Arlie has been married to his wife Norma for 35 years. His daughter, Kelly Isley, lives in Arizona with her family, and Norma's son, Ryburn McCullough, lives in Oklahoma with his family. When Arlie takes a break from traveling, he enjoys spending time with family, writing, photography, fishing, investing, church activities, and reading.

Kelly Isley is a Fortune 100 top performer who is a strategist, business leader and author with more than 20 years of experience in the aerospace, aviation, engineering, healthcare, and advertising industries.

During her career she has managed asset risk for program development, created reseller/manufacturing partnerships, executed award-winning communications programs, built profitable strategic plans, and managed operations teams for Fortune 500 companies. Her demonstrated turnaround capabilities for critical programs have focused on customers throughout Asia, Europe, North America, and South America.

Outside of the office, Kelly looks forward to spending time with her husband, family, friends and puppies. She also has a passion for photography, writing, flying, football, reading and travel.